A Key to Stonehenge

A holistic look at the relationships between Stonehenge
and the Sun, Moon and Earth, together with
the geographic siting of the monument

Robin Heath

Published by
Bluestone Press

First Edition 1993
Revised Edition 1995

- A Key to Stonehenge -

- Contents -

- A Key to Stonehenge -

- Introduction -

This book contains substantial new information about the origins and purposes of one of the world's most famous ancient buildings. Stonehenge has always attracted theories, ranging from the scientifically cautious to the downright bizarre, so why add yet one more book to the already enormous stockpile?

In an era when all the technical data concerning the motions of the Sun, Moon and Earth may be picked from a library shelf, it is refreshing to begin this work at square one, by repeating those basic observational techniques which must have been repeatedly carried out by neolithic man. We will discover that these led to certain choices and inevitable conclusions in the design, layout and construction of megalithic monuments like Stonehenge. *A Key to Stonehenge* then offers the reader a range of highly practical applications, based on scientific and astronomical truths which may readily be verified.

The book begins by showing how observations of the Sun and Moon, taken at the latitude of Stonehenge, build up into a collection of number constants - the length of the year, the timings of the lunar cycles, eclipses and so on. These numbers are immutable and the reader will discover that there are certain techniques for handling this data in order to make integrated and sensible relationships appear between the motions of the Sun, Moon and Earth. Modern man appears to have forgotten these relationships, especially with regard to his attempts to produce an integrated calendar.

The earlier constructions at Stonehenge (3300 bc to 2200 bc)* will be seen to contain all the necessary components with which to apply this basic observational data from watching the Sun and the Moon. Furthermore, an exciting and highly practical method for predicting Full Moons, New Moons and eclipses is covered in detail, enabling anyone who is interested in such things today to predict these events to high accuracy.

---

* Throughout the book, dates will be given as bc or ad in order to provide a historical datum point within the Judao-Christian culture prevalent in Europe. 0 ad is only 45 years prior to the adoption of the Roman calendar, now globally applied.

THE
moſt notable
ANTIQUITY

OF

GREAT BRITAIN,

vulgarly called

STONE-HENG

ON
SALISBURY PLAIN.

RESTORED
By INIGO JONES Eſquire,
Architect Generall to the late
KING.

LONDON,
Printed by *James Fleſher* for *Daniel Pakeman* at the ſign of the
Rainbow in *Fleetſtreet*, and *Laurence Chapman* next door
to the Fountain Tavern in the *Strand*. 1655.

The book which began the investigation into the meaning of Stonehenge in our current era: Inigo Jones' survey and restoration was undertaken in 1655, and was instigated, appropriately, by the King.
(Author's collection)

A Key to Stonehenge also takes a look at the modern calendar and demonstrates that it contains many numerical properties carried over from a much more ancient one, a calendar which arose from a natural compromise with which all calendar makers must work. It is from this compromise that a new importance emerges for the Preseli bluestone site, in West Wales.

The bluestones were evidently, to the builders, a very important aspect of Stonehenge's meaning and, unfortunately, modern man has so far been unable to share in this meaning. Whilst some specialists reckon that the bluestones arrived on Salisbury Plain courtesy of the glacial flow during the last ice-age, others maintain that the stones were quarried and then dragged and/or floated by land, river and sea all the way from Wales to Stonehenge, a direct distance of 135 miles. *How?* and *When?* have been addressed, have not been answered adequately, and somehow the all important *Why?* has been neglected.

Until now, there has been very little evidence to connect the bluestone site with Stonehenge beyond it being the source of a rather beautiful and remarkably hard granite. In *A Key to Stonehenge* may be found a coherent and completely integrated explanation as to *why* the Preseli site occupied such importance with respect to Stonehenge to the architect(s) and builders. At last there appears some hard scientific evidence for the choice of this precise location as a prime factor in the design and siting of Stonehenge.

The reader will find some very interesting geometrical solutions to astronomical problems. The mathematics is presented in such a way that even quite young adults will find no problems in understanding the meanings which underpin the theory and applications described here. Indeed, for several years I have taken young student groups and adult parties through the whole practical side of this subject without any undue problems.

To substantiate the theory here, I have taken evidence from wider sources than archaeology alone. Several centuries of archaeological endeavour still have not offered an adequate theory concerning Stonehenge, why it was built, why it was sited exactly where it is. So, in addition to astronomical facts, I have taken evidence from calendar history, geographic sitings, the Bible, folklore and what may be loosely called the ancient traditions'. Once this evidence is allowed to integrate with the archaeological and geometrical evidence, the reader will be able to build, as the book unfolds, a remarkable continuity and perspective of the motives and mental processes of a very ancient and sophisticated culture.

Contemporary with the building of Stonehenge, certain Middle East cultures produced and were using highly accurate mathematical and astronomical tables[1] Human evolution, at least in one area of the world, had already developed the

---

[1] See Evan Hadingham, *Early Man and the Cosmos*, page 13 (Heinemann). Tables to 10 places of sexagesimals (13 places of decimals) have been found on clay tablets. It is self-evident that these were not used for 'back of envelope' calculations.

3

techniques needed to understand the design rules of the Stonehenge site revealed here. Evidence of cultural interchange is suggested here although in which direction it took place remains open to question.

Finally, it has not been my aim to produce yet one more sensational text about Stonehenge. There are far too many of these already and the monument deserves better. The model I propose here involves some speculation - as all new models do - yet is very solidly underpinned by mathematical and astronomical data which any reader may verify as accurate. The significance of this theory makes Stonehenge far more wonderful than any bizarre speculations concerning extraterrestials or the supernatural. Such ill-founded material takes the credit away from those remarkable architects and astronomers who, over 5000 years ago, conceived and built the most famous megalithic monument in the world. Our ancestors *were* the builders of Stonehenge and the reader is left to decide just how much they understood concerning the planet they inhabited and which we have now inherited.

Robin Heath,
St Dogmaels, June 1993

Figure 1(a). A Solstitial Sun Alignment.
Llech y Drybedd, Moylegrove, Dyfed. The setting Sun sits on the horizon of
the sea and shines through the two small triangles into the chamber. The axis of
the monument aligns to the summer solstice sunset. (June 21st 1993; 9:40pm).
Author's photograph.

- *Sunwatching at Stonehenge* -

At the latitude of Stonehenge (a little over 51°north), the seasonal cycle of the Sun's risings and settings against the horizon is remarkable, obvious and blatantly evident to anyone living an outdoor existence. The seasons are directly caused by the axial tilt of the Earth and changes in the length of day and night together with the changes in the rising and setting positions of the Sun against the horizon are also a direct consequence of this 23.5°tilt angle. These things have changed very little since Stonehenge was built, the angular range of sunrises (and sunsets) along the horizon being about 80°.

There are so many megalithic monuments whose entrance shafts are aligned to the midwinter sunrise that one must accept that neolithic folk well understood the yearly rhythm of the Sun's risings and settings. Figure 1(b) shows this annual change, whilst figure 1(a) shows a photograph of a monument erected to face the midsummer sunset. The small triangular spaces formed between the front support stone and the two rear support stones allows the setting sun to shine into the middle chamber only during the week of the solstice. Stonehenge also has its alignment facing the midsummer sunrise, a fact known since 1721 in the current era. Solstitial alignments were thus the stock-in-trade of neolithic architecture.

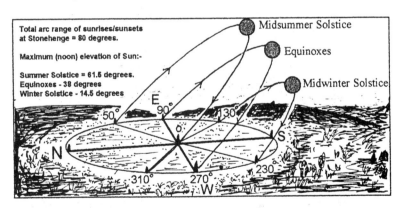

Figure 1(b). The Azimuths of Sunrise and Sunset at the latitude of Stonehenge. An observer at the marker post, in one year, sees the sunrise and sunset travel along the horizon about 40 degrees either side of the East-West equinoctial sunrise and sunset position

(Azimuth = compass bearing angle taken clockwise from true North)

It is one thing to observe and measure sunrises and sunsets at the summer and winter solstices, but quite another to assume that in 3000 bc the number of days in the solar year was accurately known and recorded. The mathematical tables impressed into clay tablets in Babylon suggest otherwise[2], but in Europe we know of no ability to count to large numbers. What we do know is that sculptures have been excavated which show pregnant women or 'goddess' figures holding crescent or lunar shaped horns inscribed with thirteen notches, these dating way back into mesolithic times[3]. These are thought to indicate a knowledge of the menstrual cycle and the monthly ovulation period which occurs about two weeks after each period. There would not appear to be a giant intellectual gap between carving 13 notches on a stick or bone and the enlarged process of recording the 365 day solar cycle. Indeed, 'artistic' solar and lunar designs incorporating relevant astronomical or even planetary data are quite widespread, even if unrecognised by conventional archaeology. Even today, primitive cultures around the globe use a 'sun-stick' for calendrical purposes; structuring time is still and probably always has been, a vital aspect of human life.

At the latitude of northern Europe, it is extremely easy to establish that 365 sunrises occur during the annual cycle of the Sun. Confirmation requires only the ability to differentiate between day and night and two cloud free sunrises (or sets) during the equinoctial periods (March 20th and September 23rd). At the equinoxes, the Sun rises almost exactly due East of an observer placed anywhere on the globe, whilst **at the latitude of southern Britain, each successive sunrise finds the Sun more than its own diameter further along the horizon.**[4] Even in relatively sunless West Wales, I have been able to make these solar observations twice in five years, using nothing more than a telegraph pole used as a foresight and positioned about a kilometre from an observing platform, appropriately provided by a neolithic burial chamber. 365 days is the number of days one observes for the year and would surely have been the number of notches on a neolithic astronomer's tally stick. If the reader requires further proof of neolithic 'art' in Europe containing repeated solar and lunar numbers as patterns and linear markings, he or she should visit the Newgrange and Knowth complex in the Boyne Valley, Ireland.

---

[2] There are many thousands of such tablets, dealing with astronomical and surveying techniques. They often run to ten decimal places of precision.

[3] An example is the famous 'Venus of Laussel', dated at around 18,000 bc. See *Goddess - Mother of living nature* by Adele Getty, page 40. (Thames and Hudson).

[4] In *The Dawn of Astronomy*, J. Norman Lockyer writes that, *"Had ignorance led to the establishment of a year of 360 days, yet experience would have led to its rejection in a few years. If observations of the Sun at equinox or solstice had been alone made use of, the true length of the year would have been determined in few years."*

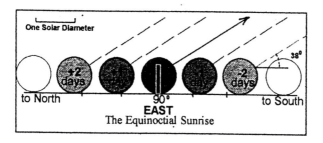

Figure 2. Successive Equinoctial Sunrises.
At the latitude of Stonehenge, an observer would see the Sun
rising like this behind a foresight marker placed directly east.
Five sunrises are shown.

Because we now know that the true length of the tropical solar year is 365 and one quarter days long, it does not follow that there are 365.25 sunrises in the year! A moment's thought will indicate the absurdity of such a statement. In truth, there are almost exactly 1461 sunrises in four years, division by 4 yielding the number of days it takes the Earth to orbit the Sun.

> ## The Earth's Orbital Period around the Sun lasts 365.2422 days

Figure 2 shows how the Sun rises around an equinoctial marker at the latitude of Stonehenge at successive sunrises. The angle subtended by the solar disc is about $0.6°$, whilst the next sunrise occurs at about $0.8°$ further northwards against the horizon, an angle which is easily measured using the most rudimentary marker. After four years of committed observation the Sun would be seen rising, on the morning of the equinox, once more, almost *exactly* over the marker, after 1461 sunrises. 365 days is the nearest whole number for the length of the year and, like it or not, we are stuck with this number. As we shall·now discover, it is rather difficult to produce a sensible calendar system using this number.

- 365 : A Mathematical Inconvenience -

365 is not a terribly useful number of days for the length of the year. To a mathematician or calendar maker, its factors (1 x 5 x 73) are dismally few and wholly inconvenient. 365 doesn't divide by 2 (for the halves of the year, summer/winter) nor will 3 or 4 (the four seasons) divide. The seven day week

hasn't got a chance here and neither can twelve months be fitted in equally within 365 days. All of which makes our present calendar, based on 365 days, rather a mess. We must dwell on this a little further, for it has a lot to tell us about Stonehenge.

The nearest number to 365 which has a range of useful factors is 364. Its factors are 1 x 2 x 2 x 7 x 13 (=364). Pausing to reflect on these factors we find that *they occur throughout our present 365-based calendar system* and it is important to find out why this is so.

We all think that there are 52 weeks in the year (4 x 13), we use a seven day week and assume that there are 4 weeks in the month (4 x 7 = 28 days). The truth is somewhat different, for 4 x 7 x 12 = 336 days and *we are missing one lunar month (29 days)* by our erroneous assumptions. Adopting the 365 day *Julian* (later *Gregorian*) calendar within a 364 based structure shoves irrational numbers all over the place. For example, within our present calendar, there are 52.142857+ weeks in the year, 4.34523+ weeks in an 'average' month and month lengths which vary from 28 to 31 days. Hardly a logical system, but then Roman numerals held back mathematics in Europe until well after 1100ad, when our present arabic numerals were (re?)introduced.

It is the ubiquitous seven day week which responsible for many of the absurdities in our Roman calendar, seven being a factor of 364 but not of 365.

- 'A Year and a Day' - The 364 day Calendar -

364 days for the year, whilst in error to astronomical realities, involves only a single day - called an *intercalary* day - to be added each year (and two every fourth year) for the calendar to align with the seasonal cycle. We are all familiar with this concept, for we add a *'leap year day'* to our present calendar every fourth year. The expression 'a year and a day' is so commonly met with throughout the folklore of Europe and elsewhere that we should investigate its origins a little further.

It turns out that until the middle ages most of Europe operated a 13 month, 364 day calendar. Although it finally faded from use around the seventeenth century, this calendar's remains have always permeated into the numbering systems of our hapless Roman calendar. It's easy to see why, for all those silly irrational numbers quoted earlier disappear when a 364 day calendar is used: 52 weeks fall exactly in the year, there are thirteen months all of 28 days in length, a season becomes exactly 91 days, 13 weeks in length (4 x 91 = 13 weeks = 364) and each week can have the traditional seven days described in the creation story of Genesis.

The origins of the 364 day calendar are obscured by the mists of time, although 'The Song of Amergin* ' and other pre-Celtic folklore, such as the various 'Tree Calendars' and the Ogham alphabet-calendar are all based on a 364 day year divided into 13 months.⁵ The pre-Christian *Book of Enoch* also describes the 364 day year in accurate and complete detail, structurally veiled as 360 + 4 in order to make it divisible by twelve months.

The 364 day calendar system probably has its roots back beyond the development of writing, because there is a working model of just such a calendar system installed in the turf on Salisbury Plain. It is called Stonehenge I and we know this to be over 5000 years old. Because modern day astronomers rarely, if ever, make fundamental observations of the motion of the Sun or Moon, it has escaped modern man's notice that such observations lead inevitably and naturally to the adoption of a 364 day based calendar system and the structure found at Stonehenge.

> **The realities of the Moon's motion in the skies inevitably supports the adoption of a 364 day calendar year.**

- ' Moonths ' - Slicing up the Year Circle -

Convenient and globally observable subdivisions of time between the day/night rhythm of the Earth's daily rotation and the longer annual cycle of the Earth's orbital period around the Sun - the year - are naturally provided by the phases of the Moon. The month (or 'moonth') reflects this useful rhythm. Although from month to month the time between each Full Moon can vary somewhat, this period, called the *lunation period*, takes about 29.5 days.

The oldest religious texts which still exist originate from India. The *Rig Veda* contains some solid and practical advice to would-be calendar makers:

"The Moon is that which shapes the years"

R.V.10.85.5

The most ancient cosmologists who left written records had acquired just enough number theory and, interestingly, just enough musical theory to harmonize the heavens with the calendar and the musical scale. Unfortunately, it is my belief, substantiated later, that they chose the one other possible contender for the length of the calendar year - 360 days - in order to achieve their

---

* *The Song of Amergin* is thought to date from 1268 bc.
⁵ For a good account of these, see *The White Goddess* by Robert Graves.

'harmonisation'. There are strong mathematical reasons for so doing, but the Moon's importance becomes much reduced.

Although the Moon's motion is highly complex, no great ability is needed to understand that there are two highly significant rhythms associated with the Moon which are evident whenever one makes observations of its motion.

The lunation period is 29.53059 days, a long term average figure. It can vary by plus or minus 6.5 hours (a *thirteen* hour range) due to many complex factors. The lunar orbital period of 27.32166 days is also a long term average figure.

The following astronomic constants should be thoroughly understood by the reader, particularly note the annual number of lunations and lunar orbits.

- The Two Lunar Rhythms -

- *The Lunation Period of 29.53059 days* -

The most observable feature of the Moon's motion is that its phases change. From New Moon to Full Moon and back again to New Moon takes about 29.53 days, and is readily observable to even the the most bleary-eyed city dweller. Each of the four phases (quarters) of the Moon thus last about 7.5 days, a number which hints at the universal adoption of a seven day week.

There are 12.368 lunations in one solar year of 365.242 days

- *The Lunar Orbital Period of 27.322 days* -

The time taken between the Moon's passage past a fixed star is called the lunar orbital period, sidereal or synodic period. It averages at 27.32 days in length, and is thus over 2 days shorter than the lunation period. Figure 3 shows how the two motions relate to each other.

The Moon makes 13.379 orbits of the Earth in one solar year

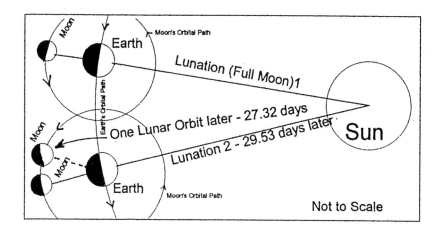

Figure 3. Why the lunar orbital period and lunation period differ.

Figure 3 tells us that lunations - the phases of the Moon - depend on the motions of both the Sun **and** the Moon, *as seen from the Earth*. The lunar orbital motion is more hidden, less obvious and needs observation of the fixed stars to confirm its rhythm; furthermore, it is independent from the Sun.

- The Two Choices, a 28 or a 30 day Month -

A 28 day month would connect a calendar straight away to a **13 month** year (28 x 13 = 364), which fits in quite nicely with what would be seen happening in the sky. Direct observation shows up the lunar zodiacal position and the position of the Sun against the circular zodiac girdle of constellations. To record these motions within a circular analogue model was the vocational calling for certain neolithic souls who were observing the Moon and the Sun at Stonehenge.

In ancient times calendar makers preferred to use a calendar which fits into the lunation period of 29.5 days. The Moon's phases offer a world-wide visual indication of the passage of time - the *weeks* and months. The nearest whole number to 29.5 is 30 days, and **12 months of thirty days** results in a 360 day year. This was the chosen numerological basis for the calendar system of the Indians, Babylonians, Egyptians and, rather latterly, the Greeks. To align a 360 day calendar to the seasons, five intercalary days must be added each year. The Egyptians added these at the four cardinal points of the solar year - equinoxes and solstices - the extra one to announce the annual inundation of the Nile Delta.

- 360 : A Mathematical Convenience -

360 is a wonderfully factorisable number - 1 x 2 x 2 x 2 x 3 x 3 x 5. It divides by all numbers up to twelve with the exception of 7 and 11. To adopt a 360 day calendar implies twelve months of 30 days. The year-circle of the Earth's passage around the Sun became *abstracted* into a calendar system which was mathematically easier. However, no calendar will ever fully integrate the difficult numbers which exist between the Sun and the Moon, just as no musical scale is perfectly harmonious. On this point, The Hindu-Greek musical scale derived from 'fitting' the thirteen note chromatic scale into the number range **360** to **720**, whilst the eight note (seven note plus octave) diatonic scale ran from **30** to **60**, with no fractional or nasty irrational numbers appearing. Musical proportions were thus made to align to events in heaven and, in an age before pocket calculators, this all seemed to harmonise remarkably well - perhaps too well.

Both 360 day and 364 day calendar systems offer sensible advantages. 360 aligns to lunation and phase timings; 364 to lunar motion through the zodiac. Unfortunately, in the modern world, we have adopted a rather less useful calendar based on 365 days - a solar dominated calendar. Despite this, we continue to use angular measurements based on 360 and a time structuring system for clocks based on 12, 24 and 60, all divisors of 360. Meanwhile, the **only** calendar system which fits in the universally-adopted-since-year-dot seven day week has sunk without trace - or nearly! Re-adoption of the 364 day calendar would allow the numbers which infuse the present calendar to integrate harmoniously - the seven day week; four week month; four seasons each of 91 days; thirteen weeks to the season and 52 week year. These things are already implied within the ludicrous 365 day calendar we inherit from the Romans; **only the thirteen month year is missing.** Why? Almost certainly because the number 13 is very much connected with the Moon and hence to matters matriarchal and the old Goddess religions. The advent of patriarchy, around 2000 bc, saw to it that all matters relating to lunar worship, and hence the Moon, were systematically and thoroughly to be eliminated from society, a process which, despite the horrors of the medieval witch-hunts, still permeates throughout western society. Our present calendar reflects this decision.*

---

* Evidence for the two choices of month length can still be found within European culture. In Britain, it is common place to use the term 'fortnight' (fourteen nights) for half the month; in France one would say ''une quinzaine' (fifteen day period). Interestingly, in Brittany, both expressions co-exist.

- Hello, Patriarchy - Goodbye, Moon -

The Age of Taurus came to an end around 2000 bc and gave way to the new Age of Aries. The vast megalith building so typical of the Taurean Age gradually dissipated as the Arien Iron Age replaced it. The patriarchs threw out the Goddess religions and with them, references to the Moon. The number thirteen became *unlucky*, and a corpus of superstitions was appended to this number in order to deter would-be witches and calendar makers from rediscovering the old 364 day calendar and other matters lunar. Thirteen months were replaced by twelve, courtesy of the 360 day Egyptian and Greek calendars and with this, around 45 ad, just before the advent of the Age of Pisces, came the adoption of the totally solar and totally irrational 365 day calendar we use today.

Thirteen *is* a very lunar number. The Moon moves *thirteen* degrees a day around the Earth. It makes just over *thirteen* orbits in a year. Thus, getting rid of the Moon meant ditching the 364 day calendar, yet a few minutes playing with a pocket calculator should convince anyone that no number other than 364 is practical or factorisable into numbers which allow some reasonable measure of integration between the apparently incompatible solar and lunar cycles. It is also apparent that our social history over the past few millenia has been reflected in our choice of calendar. I believe this to be a natural evolutionary law. Life on Earth evolved because of the complex movements of the Sun and the Moon. The seasons, the day/night cycle, the tides and weather patterns are all caused by, or depend on, the actions of the Sun **and** the Moon. To ignore either one brings imbalance.

Before we begin our visit to Salisbury Plain, we should perhaps ponder how it has come about that, in our self-professed learned and oh-so-logical civilisation, we lumber ourselves with horribly irrational calendar numbers, a time structure which uses number bases which don't fit at all within our decimal (or binary) world, a clock whose hour hand doubles the Sun's angular velocity in the sky and where almost all the wisdom passed on to us from the ancient calendar makers has been dumped along with almost everything else that mentions the Moon. Perhaps answering such questions would form a basis for understanding the apparent imbalances within western society, in which case we could do worse than to look for answers amongst the impressive remains left by that society which preceded the Patriarchs. The roots of western thought are anchored in patriarchy and this fact may be blocking our efforts to understand the minds and motives of the megalith builders.

- Moonwatching at Megalithic Sites -

All over western Europe may be found megalithic remains which were once used for accurate and systematic lunar observation. The work of the late Professor Alex Thom has furnished ample evidence of various sophisticated geometric and mathematical techniques whereby the observers at such sites were able to ascertain accurately the lunation period, the lunar orbital period and the extreme positions of the rising and setting Moon against the horizon during its 18.61 year cycle. It even appears that the minute 'wobble' or *libration* of the Moon was recorded in order to perfect the prediction of eclipses*.

This is not the right place to offer a full account of neolithic astronomy, nor is it necessary in order to understand this text. However, the reader should recognise that both lunar cycles can be easily observed and recorded with little more than a sharp eye and the ability to count or keep a tally. Both measurements demand a little ingenuity: the *exact* moment of Full Moon cannot be determined unless there is a lunar eclipse and for two months of the year, the Moon's passage past a fixed star will be obscured because the Sun conjuncts both of them - near to the time of New Moon. I believe that neolithic and bronze age astronomers faced these difficulties and found effective ways around both problems. Nowhere can this be seen more clearly than in the design and construction of Stonehenge I, which will shortly be seen to represent a perfect model of the heavens brought down to the chalk turf of Salisbury Plain.

Figure 4. Transits of the Moon.

During a 24 hour period, the Moon moves anticlockwise about thirteen degrees with respect to the stars; twenty two of its own diameters. Its motion past a chosen star every 28 days can be seen and easily measured, whence the sidereal lunar month may be found, as described in the text.

---

* See *Sun, Moon and Standing Stones* by John Edwin Wood (Oxford).

- *Making a Sun-Moon Clock* -

The most obvious way to record the lunar motion is to mark where the Moon appears in the sky when it passes adjacent to a bright star. A long stick suffices, at some distance from an observer. On the following night, at the same time (i.e. when the same star passes directly in line with the stick once again), a second stick is placed to the left of the first, marking where the Moon has moved to during the last day. The angle made between the observer and the two sticks will be found to be about 13 degrees, figure 5 showing the technique.

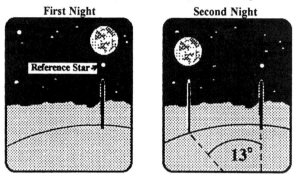

Figure 5. The Moon's daily motion (about 13°) is easily measured using a fixed reference star.

Once these two sticks have been placed accurately, then they may be used to construct a 'Moon Clock' on the ground. Taking a rope pegged at the observer, walk to the first stick. Trace the perimeter of the circle which results from this defined radius (observer to stick) and then measure the distance apart of the two sticks at the circumference. Replication of this distance will then produce a perimeter having 28 points marked on it. Moving a 'Moon marker' anticlockwise one hole each day will now emulate what is going on in the heavens.

The Moon is quite variable in the daily angle which it moves. It is fastest when New and slowest when Full, but both these extremes do not allow easy observation of the stars (there is too much light in the sky to see them). This encourages measurements to be taken at or near the time of the quarter Moons, when the daily motion is nearer to 13°. Also, if the first stick is erected directly south of the observer - a logical step used to define *south* and local noon (mid-day) through measurement of the shortest shadow - the cardinal points can be placed, and then one *always* ends up with a total of 28 markers around the circle. Within each of the four quadrant markers, as shown overleaf in figure 7, six and *only* six markers can be placed, whatever the variation from 13 degrees in the daily movement of the Moon. However roughly the initial measurement is made, the practical outcome within a cardinal point circle is always that one ends up with 28 markers around its perimeter. Thus, 28 markers define a lunar year-circle.

- Stonehenge I -
(circa 3200 - 2600 bc)

Stonehenge 1 began as an outer ditch and bank, built around 3200 bc. The bank was originally about 2 metres high and its diameter is about 90 metres. An alignment to the midsummer sunrise was provided by a pair of stones - one has vanished whilst the other has become called the *Heel Stone*.

Almost contemporary with the ditch and bank, the circular pattern of 56 Aubrey Holes was dug. Each hole was accurately spaced around the perimeter of an 87 metre diameter circle and each hole was originally about 1 metre across and 0.7 metres deep. They were apparently filled in after a very short time indeed and excavations have found bluestone chippings, remains of cremations, bones and ash. Figure 6 shows the finished construction of this first phase.

The choice of 56 holes for the Aubrey Circle would thus appear to make some connection with the minimum of 28 markers needed to construct an analogue model of just where the Moon may be located each day within the zodiac. Let us recall that the lunar orbital period is 27.32 days. 27 holes would be too few - the Moon would overshoot each month. The Sun, meanwhile, would not integrate within this 'calendar', for we must observe the 13 x 28 = 364 and move any 'Sun marker' one hole every *thirteen* days. Although the Moon would run slightly slow with 28 holes, it is possible to skip a hole or marker once in a while to correct and synchronise the Moon with its true position in the heavens.

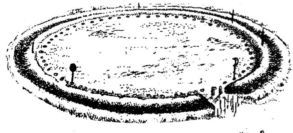

Fig 6(i)

Stonehenge I - pre-3000 bc

There may have been a wooden
building at the centre of the henge.

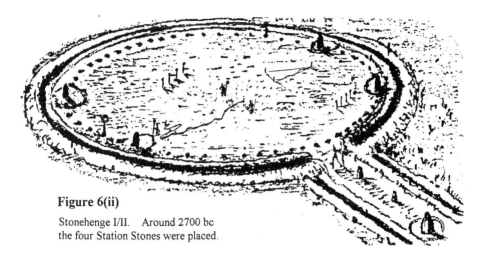

Figure 6(ii)

Stonehenge I/II.   Around 2700 bc
the four Station Stones were placed.

Figure 6. Stonehenge I, showing the 56 Aubrey Holes.
The number 56 is twice 28, and we have already seen how important
this latter number is when attempting to integrate the Moon with the
Sun within an effective calendar.

- A 28 Hole 'Aubrey' Calendar -

Let us now see how, after several thousand years, we can switch the Aubrey
'calendar' back into full operating condition. There are some very surprising
numbers which come out of such an undertaking.

Figure 7 shows how to maintain an accurate record of the motions of the Sun
and Moon by using moveable markers. The Moon marker is moved one hole
anticlockwise once a day. The Moon thus moves about *thirteen* degrees a day
and completes its circuit after 28 days.

The Sun marker has a less active life. It is also moved anticlockwise, but only
once every *thirteen* days. It is thus moved a total of 28 times during the year and
therefore to keep alignment with the seasons and astronomical reality, it must be
moved once with a *fourteen* day gap during a single circuit, rather like we adopt a
leap year day every four years in our calendar.

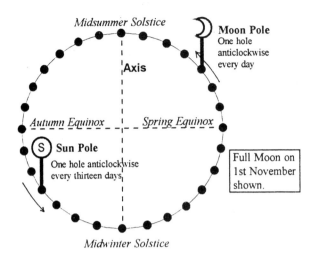

Figure 7. The Basic Sidereal Sun/Moon Calendar.
28 markers derived from a simple observation of the Moon's motion.

An integrated model of the motions of the Sun and Moon must be circular and must have 28 separate markers (or a multiple thereof) around its circumference.

This basic calendar shows the current season and the current phase of the Moon at a glance. It also shows the position of the Sun and Moon against the zodiac. It provides a very elegant and simple solution to the problem of furnishing a useful calendar, *showing at a glance the 'other' lunar rhythm (lunations), by default.*

It will not have escaped the more observant reader that the motion of the Moon with this model integrates with the diurnal rhythm of the Sun nor that the Sun is moved every 13 days, the lunar number *par excellence.* (Every 13 days the Sun is moved *thirteen* degrees). By following the less obvious and more hidden lunar orbital period (termed the *sidereal month* by astronomers), we have achieved the optimum possible measure of harmony between the 'difficult' numbers which connect the Sun, Moon and Earth in their cosmic dance.

- The Aubrey Circle -

Elegant as this may be, the Aubrey Circle possesses 56 holes, not 28, and we should ask why. An obvious response would be that, having seen how easily observations of the Moon produce a 28 marker circle, the builders decided to place an extra hole between each of the originals. The advantages of 'Mark Two' are better resolution accuracy and the possibility of 'hole-skipping' the Moon marker in order to sustain higher accuracies over long periods of time.

Figure 8 shows the Aubrey Circle set up to run as an accurate calendar. The operator's instructions hardly change - the Moon marker is moved twice a day, once at dawn and again at twilight; the Sun marker is moved one hole after 7 days and another after 6 days*. Two 7 day moves must occur at some point in the year. Alternatively, the Sun marker may be placed at one of *thirteen* lesser markers placed between each pair of holes, being moved one degree (*one day*) each day around the year-circle. The Sun thus completes his *round* in 364 days.

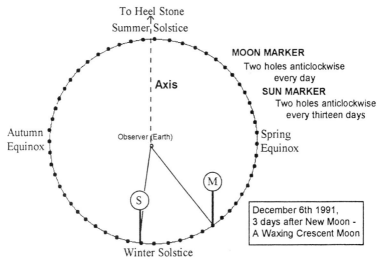

Figure 8. The 56-hole Aubrey Calendar.

The 56-hole version allows accuracy to be maintained over longer periods if the Moon pole or marker is never allowed to reside in the same hole as the Sun pole or marker. In other words, each and every New Moon, when both poles would have shared the same hole for twelve hours, the Moon pole is 'skipped' past the hole containing the Sun pole. This emulates a lunar orbital period of

---

* The ancient expression 'all at sixes and sevens' suddenly takes on a new meaning.

27.5 days and the Moon is then only slow by about 4 hours each month - two days error (four holes 'out') after a year's operation. To further improve accuracy, if the Moon is made to 'skip' a further hole each time the Sun pole passes one of the four cardinal points of the year - the equinoxes and the solstices - then the error becomes better than one hole a year (or one part in 750). This is equivalent to a clock which gains a minute every twelve hours and, just as one can reset a clock to the Greenwich 'pips', the Moon pole can always be reset opposite the Sun pole every time there is a lunar eclipse - a fairly regular occurence at Stonehenge.

The Aubrey Calendar shows at a glance the current phase of the Moon, the current season and the position of the Sun and Moon in the zodiac. It is elegant, potentially very accurate and, perhaps astonishingly, it still exists and could still be made to operate after 5000 years.

- The Inevitable 56 holes -

There is a further reason for the choice of 56 Aubrey holes. The above operator's guide could be equally well adapted to suit either a 28 hole or a 56 hole version, albeit with slight modifications. To understand why 56 holes were dug brings in a fascinating numerical relationship between the Moon's orbital period and the times in the year when eclipses are most likely to occur.

It is impossible to determine visually the exact moment of a Full or New Moon. The former event lasts for a day or two and the latter is indeterminate because the Moon disappears within the glare of the Sun. However, during an eclipse the timing can be exact - The Sun, Moon and Earth align perfectly and the time is known exactly. Total and partial lunar eclipses are not uncommon at the latitude of Stonehenge and partial ones occur at least biennially.

If the Moon's orbital plane was aligned to that of the Sun and Earth, then there would be a full blown solar and lunar eclipse each month. There isn't, becauses the Moon's orbital plane is tilted at a little over five degrees to that of the Earth. Roughly twice each year - every 173 days - a Full or New Moon will occur near to an intersection of these two planes. Providing this Full or New Moon occurs within 17 days of the intersection point, there will be an eclipse of some kind, although not necessarily visible from Stonehenge. Thus:

Eclipses can only occur during two months of each year.
(each 'month' being 34 days long, separated by about 173 days)
An 'Eclipse Year' is 346.62 days long.

These two points where the Moon's path cuts the *ecliptic* (the imaginary line which the Sun follows through the 'year-circle' of the zodiac) are termed the Moon's *nodes*; the passage of the Moon into the northern hemisphere is called the *north node* whilst that into the southern hemisphere is called the *south node*. In ancient astronomy texts, these become the *Dragon's head* and *Dragon's tail* respectively. They were given tremendous importance.

These two intersection points revolve too, moving backwards (clockwise) and taking 18.61 years to complete a circuit of the zodiac. If this is too difficult for the reader to visualise, it is because, in our sophisticated scientific age, we cannot relate the effects of this motion upon an observer on the Earth. A *geocentric* model, like the Aubrey circle, enables anyone to grasp the principles of the eclipse mechanism and thus the way in which the intersection points between the plane of the Moon's orbit and the Earth's change. Using the Aubrey calendar, for example, one cannot fail to notice that when there is a lunar eclipse, *it occurs about three holes in a clockwise direction* from the previous eclipse on a particular side of the circle. After several years of use, it would become evident that 'Eclipse markers' placed opposite each other around the circle should be moved one hole clockwise **three times each year** - thus taking 18.67 years to complete a circuit.

The mathematical elegance of this unlikely coincidence is astonishing, for 18.61 multiplied by three equals 55.83, a figure extremely close to 56 and one which enables the Aubrey calendar to readily predict eclipses. All that is needed are the two extra poles, which represent 'Danger! Likelihood of an Eclipse', placed opposite each other and which are moved clockwise three times each year. Figure 9 shows the complete Aubrey calendar/eclipse predictor; an elegant and accurate practical solution to understanding the motions of the Sun and the Moon.

56 is thus the *inevitable* choice for the number of markers around a solar/lunar analogue model. To find such a number at Stonehenge reveals an important purpose for the Aubrey holes. Interestingly, it was only the later and impressively massive developments at Stonehenge which drew John Aubrey's attention to this rather unimpressive collection of minor hollows in the ground. The Aubrey holes are thus named after this early explorer of the mysteries of Stonehenge whose first sketch plan was drawn up in the year of the Plague - 1666. Perhaps the remnants of other 28 or 56 hole circles lie waiting to be discovered at less impressive megalithic sites. The author is currently investigating a Pit Circle, near Haverfordwest, Dyfed (OS ref. SM950188), which appears to be an accurately spaced 28 hole circle.

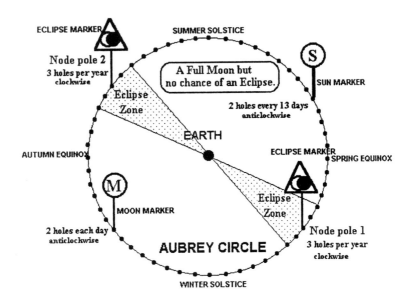

Figure 9. The Aubrey Calendar adapted for Eclipse Prediction.

Whether one feels that all of this was beyond the wit of neolithic Europeans would be a subjective and unscientific opinion because the necessary hardware evidently still exists from 5000 years ago. Furthermore, it still works and it would be very easy to restore the Aubrey calendar to its task of tracking the physical realities of solar and lunar motion. Whilst it may never be proved that men built and used Stonehenge 1 in the above described manner, it would have been even stranger for them to have laboured to produce a mindless monument - with 56 accurately placed holes within an accurate circle - which just happens to be perfectly suited to the task of accurate solar, lunar and eclipse timekeeping. Certainly, we have seen just how perfectly the monument *is* set up to perform this task, and *no number of holes other than 56 (or multiples) would suffice.*

The Aubrey circle implies the use of a 364 day year. This choice of calendar year length yields factors of 2,7 and 13, and these numbers still permeate our present calendar. But have we any more evidence to connect the 364 day year with Stonehenge? Yes!, and to discover it one needs to look at where the stones used in the construction of Stonehenge actually came from.

- The Preseli Blues -

Stonehenge I and II used stones brought from the west coast of Wales - from the Preseli mountains in what is now the county of Dyfed. They are called *Preseli Bluestones* and they formed an important part of Stonehenge's development. Many of these stones were laboriously dragged from an outcrop of rock at *Carn Menyn*, close to *Carn Meini* and *Foel Drygarn*[6] . The latitude of the site is 52 degrees or *one seventh of 364.* (The word *day* derives from *degree*, making angles and days historically inseparable - a circle perimeter represented the year and angles were thus measured in days).

There have been vague and sometimes quite illogical theories concerning a 'prototype' Stonehenge built originally in the Preseli hills. Perhaps we can now glimpse a more logical reason for such a siting at this latitude. Later, I shall be able to demonstrate why the Preseli region would have been the *only* logical choice for the site of an original monument. This must wait, for another question is begged - *why* were the bluestones taken to Stonehenge at all? It cannot have been much fun to have dragged and/or floated hundreds of megaliths from West Wales to Salisbury Plain. The shortest possible distance is 135 miles and some of those stones weighed more than 4 tons. To undertake such a Herculean task speaks eloquently about the importance those stones held to the architect(s) of Stonehenge, and we must find out what this importance was.

- The Megaliths Arrive -

The original henge-bank of Stonehenge 1 was over two metres high. Within it, the 56 Aubrey holes evenly spaced around an 87 metre diameter circle must have created a most impressive monument. The white chalk of the bank would have further enhanced the majesty of the site. Nowadays, the chalk is grassed over·and the earlier aspects of the monument are eclipsed by the massive **Sarsen Circle** and the five even more massive **trilithons** which form the inner 'horseshoe'.

The bluestones, which were moved backwards and forwards several times before finally being put to rest in circles and ellipses within the Sarsen circle and trilithon ellipse, now appear rather dwarfed by the later developments of Stonehenge III. It is these latter-day massive civil engineering projects which people associate with Stonehenge and to which they flock in their thousands from all over the world. The diagrams [figure 10(a), (b), (c) and (d)] show how

---

[6] The source of the majority of the Stonehenge bluestones was originally confirmed by Dr H.H.Thomas, a geologist and petrologist, in 1923.

the monument developed during the active 1700 years over which it appears to have been used. (For clarity, I have omitted the so-called 'Y' and 'Z' holes. A full and detailed plan of the site may be found in the excellent and low cost HMSO book *Stonehenge*.)

In order to allow for larger diagrams, figure 10(a : [i] and [ii]), showing the very first stage of Stonehenge and its development, may be found on page 16 and 17 (Figure 5).

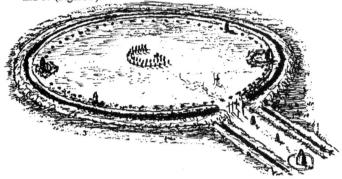

Fig 10(b). Stonehenge II with the original Bluestone concentric semicircles.

Figure 10(c). Stonehenge as it may have looked after the massive inner Trilithons were placed and the 'Y' and 'Z' holes had been dug. By this time, the Aubrey holes had, apparently, been filled in. About 1750 bc.

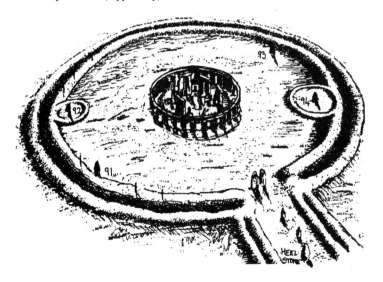

Figure 10(d). A bird's-eye view of Stonehenge, showing only the major features referred to in the text. The mounds associated with the Station Stone Rectangle are clearly visible and the relationship between this feature, the Sarsen Circle and the Aubrey Circle can be clearly seen and compared to figures 11 and 15. The Bluestones are now finally installed as two rings; one following within the Sarsen Circle and the other mimicking the ellipse of the Trilithon 'horse-shoe', having been moved backwards and forwards for at least a millenium. See figure 10(b), page 24, for their original placement within phase II.

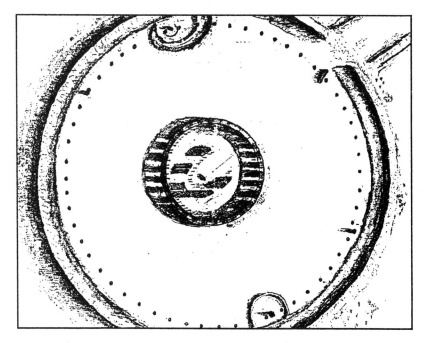

Stonehenge III - From 2100 to 1100 bc

Figure 10(a),(b),(c) and (d). The Development of Stonehenge.

From 3200 bc to 2200 bc is a very long period of time, and yet the only imposing stones erected at the monument prior to 2200 bc were the bluestone concentric semi-circles, the Heel Stone and the four *Station Stones*, of which I will have much to say later on.

- The Sarsen Circle -

The Sarsen Circle was constructed around 2100 bc. It is a quite remarkable structure, unique and enigmatic, once comprising of 30 huge upright stones arranged in a perfect circle with 30 lintels accurately interlocked and jointed to form a circular and perfectly level circular platform around the circumference. It is amply described in many textbooks and there are widespread theories concerning its original meaning. These range from stating that Stonehenge is a model of a UFO to the more probable theory that it formed a place of worship, although to whom is never made entirely clear.

We must now consider the geometry, geography, astronomy and mathematics of the Sarsen circle in the same fashion as previously for the Aubrey circle. Some very interesting results spring from this approach and they are all beautifully interconnected.

The Aubrey circle may be used to construct a seven-sided star - a heptagram - and *this contains the Sarsen circle within the 'inner star'*. Every eighth hole defines a point of the star (8 x 7 = 56) and whatever this may mean, we again find the number seven prevalent, *this time in defining the placement of the 29.7 metre diameter Sarsen circle*. Figure 11 shows the geometry of this arrangement.

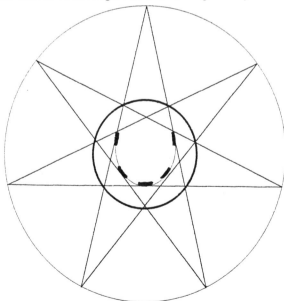

Figure 11. The Sevenfold relationship between Aubrey and Sarsen Circles.

The Sarsen circle has a circumference of 3652 *Primitive Inches*[7] , thus 10 inches represents *one day* around this impressive elevated year-circle. The primitive inch was an *Egyptian* unit of measure, equal to just over one Imperial British inch. Furthermore, the area enclosed by the Sarsen circle is *identical* with a quarter* of the Egyptian *Aroura,* a unit of area based on the **year-circle.** The French still use the unit, called an *Are,* and the *acre* derives from the same source.

Here I must make a bold assertion. The Sarsen circle contains within its physical measurements a precise statement concerning its probable cultural origins and also the astronomical reality of the true solar year of 365.24 days. It also has no truck with the 364 day year implied by Stonehenge 1, for it consisted, when originally built, of 30 upright stones and 30 lintels. Because one of the uprights is considerably smaller than the rest, perhaps these stones represented the lunation period of just over 29.5 days, **but thirty stones there were and 30 just will not go into 364.** We must find a new number system when dealing with the Sarsen circle and we have already met the only practical contender for this role - 360.

The Sarsen Circle supports the 30 day month, 12 month, 360 day calendar system.

Earlier, I showed that 364 was the nearest practical number to the dismally unfactorisable 365 solar year. 'A year and a day' was the sole mnemonic required to align seasons to calendar and the factors of 364 have survived alive and well through the ages within the weeks and months of our calendar. It is only during the last few hundred years that the thirteen month year has been finally eradicated from Europe. However, in the dim and distant past, many cultures in the Middle East thought that a 360 day calendar year was to be preferred. We have already seen why (*'A Mathematical Convenience' - page 11*).

A 360 day calendar must contain 12 months of 30 days. Once such a step is taken, the Moon's lunation period of just under 30 days then becomes the preferred lunar rhythm adopted by the calendar, although we have seen that lunations are formed by a combination of both the Sun and the Moon's apparent motion in the skies. The factors 7 and 13, which belong to the purely lunar 364 day calendar, fall useless. **The Sarsen circle is based on principles other than those upon which the Aubrey circle was constructed.** Cultural interchange, domination or imposition is evident.

---

[7] The *Primitive Inch* originates from several surveys of the Great Pyramid, where the unit may be found defining many of this building's fundamental dimensions. See *The Great Pyramid Decoded* by Peter Lemesurier (Element Books) and Appendix 2 for further information. [1 primitive inch = 1.00106 British inches.]

* The Egyptian well understood that 1461 days made up 4 solar tropical years, hence the **quarter** *Aroura.*

If further proof were needed concerning the (364) Aubrey circle and the (360) Sarsen circle, then we can readily discover it when we consider the geographical locations from where the respective stones used in each phase of construction were taken. The vast majority of the Bluestones came from *Carn Menyn*, as originally established by Dr H.H.Thomas in 1923, whilst the Sarsens were taken from a site at *Fyfield Down*, near Avebury and some 22 miles north of Stonehenge*. The following table compares the latitudes of each site and suggests that the locations from which the stones originated are directly mirroring the calendrical and numerical properties programmed into the geometrical arrangements found in phase I and phase III on the ground at Stonehenge.

- *The Lost Secret of the Stonehenge Stones* -

Latitude of the Preseli Bluestone site (Phase I and II) $= 51.95° = 364/7$
Latitude of Sarsen stone site (Phase III) $= 51.43° = 360/7$

(The sevenfold relationship shown in figure 11 mirrored in stone)

Thus the sites of the two sources of stone for Stonehenge reflect perfectly the *only* two number systems which naturally stem from any attempt to find a calendar year length with useful and practical factors.

Once the Sarsen circle is understood in mathematical terms related to the calendar, the profound differences between Stonehenge I and the later constructions of Stonehenge III become as obvious as their differences in scale and magnificence. If we consider the Aubrey and Sarsen circles together, we can discover useful information about the way in which the lunation period and the lunar orbital period interact with each other. This astronomical relationship has already been illustrated in figure 3; we now turn to the two constructions on the ground at Stonehenge to discover a further correlation.

Figure 12 shows the two concentric circles (not to scale). Over 800 years separates their building - they have only co-existed since about 2200 bc. We shall use the Moon position marker on the Aubrey circle and a lunation indicator on the Sarsen circle to indicate Full Moons. This latter marker moves one megalith anticlockwise each day. When it reaches the shorter stone (which perhaps indicated half a day) we have reached the next Full Moon, after 29.5 days, and the marker is made to return to its starting position immediately,

---

* I am grateful to the custodians of the Alex Keiller (Avebury) Museum, Dave Davridge and Mike Powell for assistance in pin-pointing the exact site of the Sarsen stones, agreed by archaeologists and geologists. Also for running a wonderful museum - far better than anything at Stonehenge.

without waiting for the remaining half day. In other words, one circuit is made to take 29.5 days in order to simulate lunations. As the 56 hole Aubrey Calendar already requires a Moon marker to be moved every half day, this suggested technique would not have caused the lifting of any eyebrows, although it does not square at all well with the older Aubrey calendar, because lunations are no longer geometrically, astronomically or calendrically related to the Sun's position in the zodiac.

After the Aubrey Moon marker has completed one revolution of the 56 Aubrey holes, in accordance with the instructions already given, the lunation marker falls about, but not exactly, two megaliths short of one revolution. The thirty stones (29 plus one very much thinner upright) form an approximate tally for the 29.5 day lunation period whilst the circular platform of lintels, which was made perfectly level, could have been used to mark the *exact* angular position of the current Aubrey Moon marker. If this action was repeated for each lunar orbit, the result, after one solar year, would be that the Sarsen circle would be marked with 13 equal divisions plus a remainder of about 0.4 of these divisions. In other words, the 13.379 lunar orbital periods within the year would be equally placed, as marks, *correctly dated and in chronological order* around the perimeter of the top of the Sarsen circle. This platform would be divided up into 13.379 angular sections.

Now: the Sarsen circle has a perimeter of 3,652 primitive inches and thus appears already 'calibrated' or divided into the days of the year. The lunar sidereal months are thus shown within the days of the year (10 primitive inches corresponding to one day). This method of extracting the sidereal lunar period by superimposing it on the Sarsen circle, itself a perfect dimensional representation of the Egyptian year-circle, is both eminently practical and necessary for astronomical prediction work.

Working this 'clock' the other way, to find the number of lunations in the solar year, one notes where the Aubrey Moon marker - which 'overshoots' a revolution - ends up following each lunation, again by placing angular marks on the platform above the Sarsen circle. This eventually divides the 'year-circle' into 12.4 lunar months - the annual lunations are directly obtained, once again *already calibrated to the days in the year.*

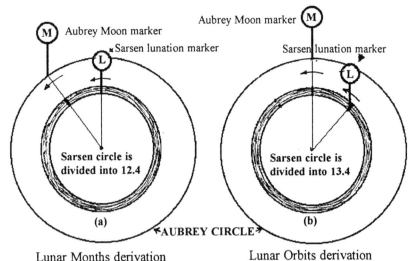

Lunar Months derivation   Lunar Orbits derivation

Figure 12. Interelationships between Aubrey and Sarsen Circles.

> The mathematics and geometry of this procedure are simple enough. 29.5/27.3 gives 1.0806. After one lunation, the Moon marker has 'overshot' by 0.0806 of a revolution. This represents 29 degrees, or 1 / 12.4 of a circle. Taking the numbers the other way round, 27.3/29.5 gives 0.925. After one lunar orbit, the lunation marker has 'undershot' by 1 - 0.925 of a revolution. This amounts to 0.075 of a circle, or 26.84 degrees - 1 / 13.4 of a circle. Taken together, these two divisions of the Sarsen circle yield the two lunar periods.

This technique would have allowed the two lunar time constants to have been related to the days of the year directly and simply. By laying a rope around the perimeter of the Sarsen circle platform, the 'age' (phase) and the position of the Moon against the zodiac could have been found for any given day of the year. I shall deal more fully with this technique in a later section but, for the moment, the reader is asked to consider why the Sarsen circle dimensions are just what they are, and whether or not the placing of the above mentioned angular marks would have been facilitated if the whole circular platform had once been covered over, allowing access to the centre of the monument, essential for accuracy using this technique.

A certain Mr R.F.Brinckerhoff[8] discovered marks on the top face of the Sarsen lintels, which are more level than the ground upon which the Sarsen circle is built on. This remains scant evidence, because most of the lintels are no longer present on site for us to inspect. However, using a model of the Aubrey and Sarsen circles, I was able to predict lunations and the return of the Moon

---

[8] Brinckerhoff,R.F., 'Astronomically orientated markings on Stonehenge', Nature, 263, 465-9 (1976).

past a fixed reference star in the zodiac to better than 6 hours, one year in advance. The only other way of attempting such a feat, using hardware at Stonehenge, would be to 'fast forward' the Aubrey markers, although these are limited to a resolution of 12 hours or so. For eclipse prediction, as we shall see, this is not adequate to discover whether or not a lunar eclipse will be visible at the location - it may occur during the daytime. Chinese astronomers were systematically executed for failing to predict a visible eclipse and with that sort of threat hanging over them, it is perhaps understandable that ancient astronomer/priests wanted to perfect their craft.

Stonehenge III, at least the Sarsen circle part, formed a circular 365 day year, 29.53 day lunation based calendar whilst the Aubrey holes were designed for systematic and accurate scientific observations of the positions of the Sun and Moon in the sky and, as we have seen, such a design has to follow the 27.32 day lunar orbital period - a 364 day process. The interactions of the Sun and the Moon markers around the Aubrey circle only indicated lunations incidentally, although very elegantly and quite automatically.

Because 800 years separated the two phases of construction at Stonehenge, it is hardly surprising that the requirements of the culture changed during the period. It is also interesting that, in the view of many of our top astro-archaeologists, neolithic and Bronze Age astronomy never evolved, it steadily degenerated so that, by about 1600 bc, the party was over and the great achievements of our ancestors were consigned to history, forgotten and left for forthcoming generations to re-discover. Because no written records exist from the period, the only 'hard' information we now have access to are the monuments themselves, their geometry and their alignments to significant astronomical events. But we do have some other sources of information too, however unscientific and woolly these may appear. Folklore, legends and myths all speak eloquently of events long ago, and when, as often happens, the story is embellished with certain numbers, then these can and do offer clues which allow us to catch a fleeting glimpse of what appears to have been going on in pre-Roman Britain. It is to these sources that we must now turn our attention.

Pentre Ifan (52°N ; 4° 46' W).
This magnificent monument is situated just below *Carn Ingli*, Welsh for *Cairn of the Angels* (visible in background). It lies less than four miles from the bluestone outcrop at *Carn Menyn* and may date back to 3500 bc.
[*photograph*: - Richard Heath]

- The Battle of the Calendars -

- *The Swan-song of the Goddess* -

The third millenium bc marked the beginning of what is called the patriarchal era. The earlier matriarchal cultures were gradually superseded by male dominated ones. In nearly all cultures in the world the Sun is regarded as a masculine archetype or deity whilst the Moon is seen as representing the feminine archetype or deity, for reasons which áre well explained in any book of modern psychology or mythology. The building of Stonehenge III with its implied twelve 'solar' months more or less synchronised with this changeover from matriarchal to patriarchal values.

Perhaps there really was a 'Battle of the Calendars' as European folklore suggests. The *Song of Amergin* dates from about 1260 bc and describes a thirteen month calendar, where each month is represented by a tree and where the extra day - the winter solstice - is described in terms thus : *"Who but I knows the secrets of the unhewn dolmen?"* This Irish text was created in the very country which holds the most remarkable burial chamber in Europe, whose unhewn stones still mark the solsticial sun's rays by illuminating the central chamber. Newgrange, with its spiral carvings and quartz coverings, is one of the wonders of the ancient world. The text poses difficult astronomical questions to the reader (*"Who but myself knows where the Sun shall set?"* and *"Who foretells the ages of the Moon?"*).

The *Song of Amergin* contains frequent references to the numbers 7 and 13. The calendar it describes is clearly a 13 month, 364 day one with a single intercalary day to align to the seasons - chosen to fall on the day of the winter solstice, currently within two days of our Christmas holy-day. 28 days there must be in each month and this connects the poem directly to the sort of activity we have shown to be going on at Stonehenge before 3000 bc.

The ever popular and charming fairy story *Briar Rose,* otherwise known as *The Sleeping Beauty,* has encrusted within its plot the mathematics of the twelve versus thirteen conflict, relating this to a prophetic warning against neglect of the feminine, and hence lunar, qualities of life. Like all good fairy tales, the awakening of the sleeping princess by the kiss of the charming prince heralds a 'happy ever after' marriage and restoration of the decayed kingdom. Here is a theme of unification between the male and female aspects of life following a period of disregard of the feminine component. For those not familiar with the story, the trouble all starts when the king plans to invite all the wise women of his kingdom to a banquet to celebrate the birth of his daughter. Unfortunately, he has to refuse an invitation to the *thirteenth* wise woman of the land because he only has *twelve golden* plates. She then bursts in, uninvited and unwelcome, and places the predictable curse on the princess and the kingdom.

The pre-Christian *Book of Enoch* describes fully the celestial mechanics of the 364 day calendar. It is known as *1 Enoch* by scholars in order to distinguish it from the post-Christian 'translation' discovered last century and which is known as *2 Enoch*. This later text replaces the 364 day with the 365 day calendar and introduces several gross mathematical errors in the process, attempting to make the old calendar fit the new one. The author of *2 Enoch* fails utterly to remove the constant repetition of the number seven within the original text.

Whatever these ancient texts have to tell us, it is from the same theme of solar versus lunar, 12 versus 13 and male versus female that any modern revisionist of the calendar must work. A **true** calendar must attempt to integrate, as far as is possible, the apparently incompatible numbers of the Sun and Moon.

No calendar does this perfectly, although we have seen that the one on Salisbury Plain does it infinitely better than the rest.

I believe that the ancient cultures of the world wrestled with this problem just as perhaps we should today. Their suggested solutions are still to be found right under our feet, because of their enduring monuments of stone. After many centuries of research, neither the scientific world nor anybody else has delivered a satisfactory explanation for megalithic architecture which would enable us to compare the apparently primitive status of ancient Europeans with their well organised and profoundly impressive monuments. The tendency in the past has been for archaeologists to take a very cautious view of any apparent technical achievements and to play up the contents of grave, bell barrow and tumulus as proof of a *'nasty, brutish and short life'* for tribesmen in ancient Britain. In truth, astro-archaeology has blown a rather big hole in the well defended walls of this thesis during the last 30 years. Even today, we find within the British Isles regions where frequent killing, destruction, illness and death occur cheek by jowl with centres of academic excellence and scientific research. In our times, these two facets of life coexist at the same place and time and it would be rather unscientific to assume that this same state of affairs could not have prevailed in 3000 bc - but just *who* were these astronomer/priests?

My suggested approach for unlocking the secrets of Stonehenge is to widen the axioms under which we analyse the data. Conventional scientific thinking cannot embrace the use of the Sun and Moon in their symbolic roles. The rules of the game haven't allowed mythology, folklore and calendar history, nor can they permit the existence of long-rotted Sun and Moon poles without physical evidence - which will never be found in a month of lunar eclipses. Similarly, I would ask the reader, particularly if he or she has the benefit of a modern scientific training, to accept that in neolithic and bronze age times, early man clearly strove to achieve accuracy yet may not have always realised it. For this reason, measurements and dimensions *to within one percent accuracy* will be brought into the arena as supporting any particular intention neolithic astronomers appear to have had.

We shall now undertake an analysis of Stonehenge where the axioms are suitably widened, not at the expense of scientific thoroughness but in order to show what the monument is trying to tell us about life on the Earth. This approach will prove to be spectacularly successful in shedding new light on the mysteries of Stonehenge.[9]

---

[9] Some scientists use the 'accuracy excuse' to dismiss important connections at megalithic sites which are not accurate to umpteen decimal places. This is rather unfair: for example, Kepler's laws of planetary motion are only approximate due to orbital interactions between each planet and yet to dismiss the usefulness of Kepler's laws would be sheer folly. And no plant or tree grows *exactly* to the Golden Section number *phi*, yet life carries on and evolves regardless. We are dealing with statistical probabilities and mean values.

- *Chapter Two* - The Station Stone Rectangle -

- The Harmony of the Triangles -

Lying symmetrically across the axis of Stonehenge I are the four Station Stones - numbered 91 to 94 on the HMSO plan. They form an accurate rectangle whose sides are in the numerical ratio 5:12. Symbolically, such an arrangement is satisfying, for the Sun reaches its most northern point in the year against the horizon at the summer solstice and the '12' sides of the rectangle simulate the position on the Earth of the tropics of Capricorn and Cancer. Straight away, one can find a parallel between this rectangle, the Aubrey circle and the realities the Earth holds with the Sun (figure 13). The octagonal shape implied from the axis of symmetry can be seen to represent our planet. The axis azimuth, which coincides with the latitude of Stonehenge, marks the most northerly annual sunrise at this latitude - the annual midsummer sunrise which causes so much conflict at Stonehenge between new age folk and the police. The similarity between the Earth and Stonehenge is thus clearly seen - the monument mimics our planet in a quite astonishing manner.

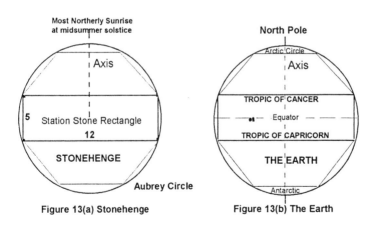

Figure 13. Links between Stonehenge I and the Earth's axial tilt.

Models of Stonehenge.

The top photograph shows the author's Aubrey calendar with a removeable scale model of the Sarsen Circle and associated later phases in the centre. It has predicted eclipses to the day for the past six years, and many larger versions are in use throughout the world. The second model - bottom photograph - has been mounted on a 51 degree angle, an artificial 'Sun' simulating sunrises and sunsets throughout the year without the need to be on-site at Stonehenge, something which is almost impossible now the site is so heavily defended.

We must take a further look at this link between the Stonehenge site and the planet we inhabit. Professor Alex Thom spent years of his life investigating commonalities of units of length to be found throughout European megalithic sites. After decades of critical analysis, it appears as if the so-called *Megalithic Yard* (MY) formed a common unit. Thom defined this unit as being 0.829 metres in length, making the Aubrey circle diameter equal to 104 MY. This number is equal to the product of 13 and 8: the octagon and the Aubrey calendar shout out these two numbers.

We have just seen that the planet Earth holds a signature of the number 8, through the placing of the Tropics and Arctic circles - these fundamental latitudes being created due to the Earth's axial tilt. The number 13 has been seen throughout chapter one to relate to matters lunar whenever we have encountered it. Both these numbers are consecutive members of the Fibonacci series, a numerical series which may be found throughout most evolutionary processes. Between the Earth and the Sun, and seen from the Earth, the planets Mercury and Venus trace out orbital paths which retrograde three and five times respectively in their zodiacal circuit. 3 and 5 are the next two lower numbers of the Fibonacci series. In my book, *Sun, Moon, Man, Woman*, (privately published in 1992), I show that, seen from the Earth, **all** the planets fit into the Fibonacci series and hence that the planets can be understood as an evolutionary series where: - Mercury = 3; Venus = 5; Earth = 8; Moon = 13; Mars = 21; Jupiter = 34; Saturn = 55; Uranus = 89; Neptune = 144 and Pluto = 233.

Planetary Law : Viewed from the Earth, the retrograde angle and motions of the planets follow the Fibonacci series, this being derived from division of the zodiacal circle, if and only if the Earth is allocated the number 8 and the Moon the number 13 within the series.

As the Fibonacci series grows, the ratio between consecutive terms approaches *phi*, the Golden Section number*, the quintessential number of evolution. The dimensions built into Stonehenge and the numbers built into the Aubrey calendar appear to align with the law stated above.

Dr Gerald Hawkins' seminal work, *Stonehenge Decoded*, (Doubleday, 1964) opened up the importance of the Station Stone rectangle. Hawkins showed that the solar and lunar alignments found within the rectangle **could only occur within half a degree of the chosen latitude of Stonehenge.** Astronomically, it turns out that Stonehenge is sited in the middle of a very narrow band of

---

* *Phi* = 1.618033989..., The Fibonacci series runs 0, 1, 1, 2, 3, 5, 8, 13, 21, 34, 55, 89, 144, 233 etc, where each term is formed from the addition of the two preceding terms - starting with 0 and 1. Division of two consecutive terms of the series yields -*phi*. 1/*phi* = 0.618033989... = 1 - *phi*, a unique reciprocal!

latitudes - less than 1° - where the astronomical alignments shown in the figure below permit the four stones to take a precise rectangular shape. If Stonehenge had been built north of Oxford or on the Isle of Wight, the shape becomes a parallelogram - and it could not have been fitted around the perimeter of the Aubrey (or any other) circle. These alignments are shown in figure 14.

Because the Moon's orbital plane is angled at just over five degrees to that of the Sun and Earth, the Moon does not rise and set with the same annual angular range as the Sun. At Stonehenge, the range of solar rising and settings is confined within two arcs of about 80° but the *extremes* of lunar rising and settings can occur over a larger arc - the maximum summer moonrise occurs at 90° to the winter sunset and the summer sunrise at 90° to the maximum winter moonset. Such a relationship connects Sun and Moon through right angles *only* at the latitude of Stonehenge, hence the rectangle and *our continuing discovery of the uniqueness of the siting of the monument on our planet.*

These facts, with other alignments, led Hawkins to analyse every possible alignment at Stonehenge using the then remarkable new IBM computers. His book was blasted by the establishment. "Moonshine over Stonehenge" was how the late Professor Richard Atkinson[10] headed his attack on Hawkins' theories. In fairness, this same learned man supported Hawkins in his quest for accurate information concerning the history and dating of the various phases of the monument. In true scientific tradition, he assisted even when he failed to agree with the conclusions, as he also did with the Thom survey and researches.

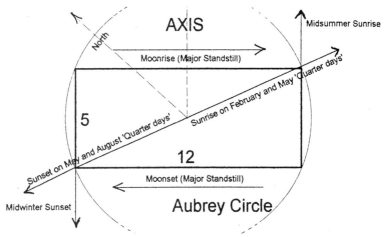

Figure 14. Solar and Lunar Alignments made by the Station Stone Rectangle *(after Hawkins).*

---

[10] R.J.C.Atkinson, Stonehenge, Pelican 1979. The definitive textbook concerning the archaeology of the monument. Highly recommended.

The Station Stone rectangle, with an added diagonal, forms two right angled triangles whose sides are in the ratio 5:12:13. Figure 15 shows the arrangement. A 5:12:13 triangle is one of a set of right angled triangles whose sides are in whole number ratios. They are termed *Pythagorean triangles* although they were known about and their properties used millenia before the Greek philosopher. These triangles have a unique property, **The square on the hypotenuse (longest side) equals the sum of the squares on the other two sides.** Thus, in the most commonly known 'Pythagorean' triangle, the so-called 3:4:5 triangle, five squared (25) equals three squared plus four squared (9 + 16). For the 5:12:13 triangle, 169 = 144 + 25 and the apex angle of the triangle is 22.6 degrees, which is less than one degree from the Earth's axial tilt angle (currently 23.45°, but varies with a 41,000 year period from 21° to 24.5°). An octagon can be formed from sixteen 5:12:13 triangles.

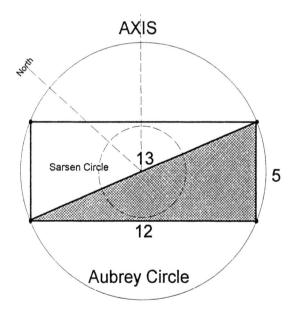

Note that the Sarsen Circle is just enclosed by the rectangle.

Figure 15 . The 5:12:13 Triangle formed from a diagonal of the Station Stone Rectangle.

- Five, Twelve, Thirteen -

The numbers twelve and thirteen should by now hold considerable meaning for the reader. They suggest something far more than just numbers and we may now suppose that they may suggest the Sun(12) and the Moon(13), the archetypal Male and Female qualities. But what about the number five, juxtaposed between them with this triangle?

In many ancient cultures, alchemic texts, folklore and Pythagorean traditions, the number five represented generic Man, the unified being created "*in the image and likeness of God, male and female created he(?) them*". (Genesis, Chapter One, vs 26). Five was seen as the number of health, harmony and consciousness. The *pentagon* and its brother, the *pentagram star* form a most ancient 'occult' symbol. In modern geometrical terms this shape links the number five with *phi* to a remarkable extent. Five also linked the integration of the male with the female qualities and thus became associated with marriage - numerology and Hindu musical theory identifying the number 2 as being the first *female* number, whilst 3 represented the first *male* number. However strangely such ideas fall on modern ears, we might do well to remember that the most harmonious interval in music is the *tonic* or keynote played with the *fifth* or *dominant* note of the scale, and that the relative frequencies or string lengths of these two notes form an exact ratio 3:2.

Symbolically, Man, as the highest consciousness currently on the Earth, stands as the mediator between the Sun and the Moon in this the 5:12:13 triangle and it was from this symbolic and musical information, and working with plans of Stonehenge* , that I first stumbled on a most interesting truth:-

---

Dividing the '5' side of a 5:12:13 triangle into the ratio 3:2 produces a point from which can be drawn a new hypotenuse whose length is 12.369, the *exact* number of lunations in one solar year.

The resulting triangle holds a profound truth concerning the astronomy of the Sun, Moon, Earth system, for here we have been able to arrange a geometrical 'marriage' of the Sun and the Moon, one which integrates symbolic material and astronomical realities, numerology, astrology and musical science. Symbolically, *all* is exactly as it should be. The female '2' comes down from the feminine and lunar '13' side; the male '3' comes up from the masculine and solar '12' side of the triangle.

---

* I am indebted to Dr A.S.Thom for giving me the 1:250 plan which he and his father produced during his 1973 survey of Stonehenge.

- The Lunation Triangle -

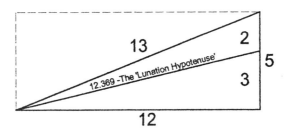

Figure 16. The 5:12:13 Lunation Triangle - with *'lunation'* hypotenuse.

The point where the male meets the female - the point of integration or balance - is the sole point at which one can construct a 'lunation hypotenuse' whose length corresponds exactly to the number of lunations in the year. We have already discovered that lunations are a product of both the Sun's and the Moon's motion and this triangle enables anyone to produce *a length* corresponding to the annual number of lunations - an awkward 12.368 - without having to deal with fractions or decimals. It is produced directly, **as a length already correctly proportioned to the '12' and '13' sides.**

The 5:12:13 triangle, interpreted in this logical, symbolically, astronomically and historically valid way, contains the secret of the 'sacred marriage' of the Sun and the Moon, and hence offers one solution to the timeless problem of human integration. It also enables simple and highly accurate calculations of lunar phases.

This geometric technique reveals an astronomical fact to extreme precision, the resulting length is **within 0.008% of the average lunation figure!!** There *are* 12.368 lunations in the solar year, this triangle offering us 12.369. The discovery of the lunation triangle represented a scientific achievement on a par with the discovery of the calculus for, armed with this technique, an astronomer can readily predict eclipses to accuracies of better than a few hours, years in advance (see the appendices for more details on accuracies and techniques). Later on in this book the reader will be able to see how to apply this information, using neolithic technology.

To anyone interested in calendar production, eclipse prediction or an accurate understanding of Full and New Moons, this triangle represents a major step forward. In effect, **knowledge of this geometric function provides a superb tool for astronomers.** Modern practitioners have lost the secret, all that remains are the numerological, musical and mythological crumbs, although the fact that there is a 5:12:13 triangle slap-bang in the middle of Stonehenge offers some stone-hard evidence that the builders were capable of building a highly accurate rectangle containing two 5:12:13 triangles. Why? Were the solar and lunar alignments at the location of Stonehenge reason enough, or did the architect know something we have long since forgotten? Let us now look at other evidence which will shed light on further evidence that there was, indeed, ancient knowledge of the lunation triangle.

- *The Draught of Fishes* -

In any modern Bible, the twenty first chapter of the gospel of St John - the so-called *appendix* to the gospel - will be found an accurate description of the symbolic, mathematical and geometrical function and purpose of the lunation triangle. Because the Bible is not found in every home these days, it will be necessary for me to quote the story below, allowing the reader to fully comprehend the lightly encrypted information being given within the context of a metaphysical text. Despite translations through the ages, the story has survived intact and is completely transparent as to its astronomical meaning. I have omitted verses from the story which are not directly relevent.

1. "After these things Jesus shewed himself again to the disciples at the sea of Tiberias; and on this wise he shewed himself.
2. There were together Simon Peter and Thomas called Didymus, and Nathanael of Cana in Galilee, and the sons of Zebedee, and two other of his disciples.
3. Simon Peter saith unto them, I go a fishing. They say unto him, We also go with thee. They went forth, and entered into a ship immediately; and that night they caught nothing.
4. But when the morning was now come, Jesus stood on the shore: but the disciples knew not that it was Jesus.
5. Then Jesus saith unto them, Children, have ye any meat? They answered him, No.
6. And he said unto them, Cast the net on the right side of the ship, and ye shall find. They cast therefore, and now they were not able to draw it for the multitude of fishes.
7....
8. And the other disciples came in a little ship;(for they were not far from land, but as it were two hundred cubits), dragging the net with fishes.
9 and 10 ......
11. Simon Peter went up and drew the net to land full of great fishes, an hundred and fifty and three: and for all there were so many, yet was not the net broken.
12 and 13 ......
14. This is now the third time that Jesus shewed himself to his disciples, after that he was risen from the dead."

Jesus, the **thirteenth** member and the saviour of the group of **twelve** disciples, admonishes **five** named disciples (and **two** un-named ones) to cast their net on the right side of the ship. Which is the *right* side of a ship* - is this the right angle being described? The number 153, for the number of fishes caught, is unique to this chapter of the Bible and occurs only in the above passage. So what, you may ask? Try this:-

---

153 is the square of 12.369, the number of lunations in the year. To find the arithmetic length of the hypotenuse of the lunation triangle one must use Pythagoras' theorem, whence

$$(\text{hypotenuse})^2 = 3^2 + 12^2$$
$$= 9 + 144$$
$$= 153$$
$$\text{hypotenuse} = \sqrt{153} = 12.369$$

Two hundred cubits** (a Hebrew long or sacred cubit was 25 inches long) corresponds to 5000 inches. The numbers 2, 3 and 5 interplay throughout this story. It was the **third** time that Jesus appeared to his disciples. The number of disciples in the boat will be found to contain the numbers 3 and 2, albeit somewhat encrypted.

This story is a remarkably coherent and well preserved account of the function of the 5:12:13 triangle embedded within another story - a metaphysical text. That it links the Christian message with something found on the ground at Stonehenge may, at first, seem very strange indeed and yet the message of the triangle is that same one of harmony and unity, the coming together of the male and female aspects into a 'marriage'. The Christian message holds the human implications and carries the 5:12:13 triangle along as astronomical cargo, although both carry the same symbolic content, and a further and most spectacular example may be found where both messages appear interlinked. Previously, I have shown that the *latitude* of Stonehenge is unique: now we will discover that the *longitude* is similarly locked, answering the age old question - **why is Stonehenge sited *exactly* where it is?** We shall also be able to suggest why the Preseli Bluestone site was so important to the architects?

---

* In English one would say *Star*-board, originating from *steer-board*, but both words derive from Old English (*steorra* and *steor* respectively).

** The radius to side length of a regular octagon is 200:153.

- *The Stonehenge-Preseli Lunation Triangle* -

Consider the following statement:

> **The Siting of Stonehenge is such that it forms, with the Preseli Bluestone site and the respective lines of latitude and longitude, a huge *lunation triangle* across southern England and Wales.**

Using spherical geometry, it is readily shown that this huge triangle is accurately represented on the ground, mimicking the one found within the Aubrey circle. Lundy Island contains the exact site of the right angle, and Caldey Island, just off the coast at Tenby, contains the site of the 3:2 point. Lundy and Caldey thus form, with the Preseli bluestone site and Stonehenge, all the four points needed to define a huge lunation triangle. Figure 17 shows this triangle.

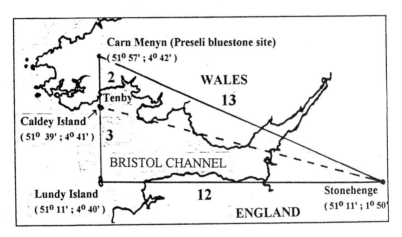

Figure 17. The Stonehenge - Preseli Lunation Triangle.

It follows that the relationship between the *only* two large islands in the Bristol Channel are linked to the Preseli site by distances exactly on the same north-south meridian and which are separated by the ratio 3:2. This is strange material indeed, especially when one further considers that both the islands and the Preseli bluestone site sport ancient remains dating back to at least 8000 bc. What fascinates me even more is the fact that the ancient name for Tenby is *Dinbych y Pysgod*, Welsh for 'City of the Fish'. This is, indeed, an appropriate name for an ancient Christian settlement lying on the 3:2 point, the 'Christ-point' of unity, on this huge 5:12:13 triangle.

It inevitably follows that if the 'Stonehenge-Preseli Triangle' is other than a quite remarkable coincidence then Stonehenge was sited uniquely *after* the builders discovered the remarkable and exact north-south alignment of the two islands. Presumably, they would then have measured the 3:2 ratio to the Preseli site, taking the stones from this venerated site all the way to Stonehenge. If this be the case, then we have at last the reason why Stonehenge is sited exactly where it lies, locked in latitude and longitude lines which each carry a profound meaning. Stonehenge was built *exactly* east of Lundy Island and was the final and not the first stage in this geometric statement.

The difficult question to now answer is how it becomes possible for this triangle, which is so clearly used as the basis for an early Christian text, to have existed 3000 years before the time of Jesus. The Gospel of St John was written at least 3000 years after the the choice of site for Stonehenge and at least 2700 years before the placement of the Station Stone rectangle, which makes ourselves nearer to St John than he was to the builders of Stonehenge. Where did the writer get his information from? Did the Christian story become appended onto another, much older realisation concerning the symbolic and astronomic secret held by the lunation triangle? Was this triangle common knowledge to several civilisations? If so, then we can no longer say that Stonehenge is/was an independent cultural artifact. One way or another, the monument reflected something which was written into the religious texts of our era. **There must have been cultural interchange, although not necessarily during neolithic times.**

The Stonehenge-Preseli triangle must have been conceived from consideration of the only two fixed points which it contains - the two islands of Lundy and Caldey. Both have names which should ring a few bells to students of the past and both were important sites to early Christian settlers. It must be apparent that they enjoyed importance many thousands of years previous to this and, if I were an archaeologist, I would want to dig there rather than almost anywhere else in Europe.

I recognise that my thesis concerning the lunation triangle is very strange material indeed, but one cannot wriggle away from the facts presented here. Those two islands have always been fixed points (even if once they were not engulfed by the sea); the ratios, lines of latitude and longitude and certainly Stonehenge itself are now also fixed, immutable and there for all to see and measure on the ground. And together these things form a lunation triangle. Once our vision is widened beyond the Stonehenge site, we discover something very important about ancient cultural aspirations. Are we glimpsing here aspects of *The Perennial Philosophy* or *The Ancient Wisdom*? We turn to Egypt for one possible answer.

- *The King's Chamber and the Queen's Chamber* -

The Great Pyramid of Cheops is probably the most surveyed building in the world. Every dimension and angle has been scrutinised by expert and crank alike in order, often, to elucidate whatever theory the interpreter has wished to pursue. It is, at one and the same time, a King's tomb - although no body has ever been found there, a prophesy of human evolution, an encoded message about the purposes of human life and many other theories, some so bizarre as to be tiresome. However, be that as it may, numerical facts arising from the many surveys furnish accurate mathematical and geometrical relationships integral to this remarkable structure, which was built around 2650 bc - well after the Aubrey circle of Stonehenge I.

The number 153 may be found here, at many places within the building[11] . *From the summit platform, at masonry course 202, there are 153 masonry courses to the base of the King's Chamber.* One may be forgiven for thinking this to be a coincidence, until one discovers that there are 179 courses to the base of the Queen's Chamber. *179 happens to be the square of the number of lunar orbits in the year - 13.379.*

Doubly interesting is the fact that the King's chamber - which surely has something solar about its name - suggests the number relating to the Sun/Moon phenomenon which is caused by the Sun and its light - the lunation process , whilst the Queen's chamber - which is feminine and hence lunar - suggests the number relating to a purely lunar phenomenon - the annual number of lunar orbits. I decided to pursue this matter further by investigating whether or not a similar triangle, relating to the lunar orbital period, existed in addition to the 5:12:13 lunation triangle, but using the purely lunar numbers 13 and 14, which we discovered permeating the Aubrey calendar. There is. The lunation triangle is not a fluke nor a coincidence - it may be extended and developed. It forms part of a cosmology based around whole numbers and the right-angled triangle.

- *The Lunar Orbit Triangle* -

> **A right angled triangle may be constructed using the two lunar numbers 13 and 14. Dividing the third side into the ratio 3:2 produces an intermediate hypotenuse whose length is 13.379 - the exact number of lunar orbits in a solar year.**

---

[11] *The Great Pyramid Decoded* - see previous reference.

This is a remarkable development, for within the two triangles one may find nearly all the information an astronomer needs to understand fully the way in which the Sun, Moon, Earth system interacts. The lunar orbit triangle is shown below (figure 18).

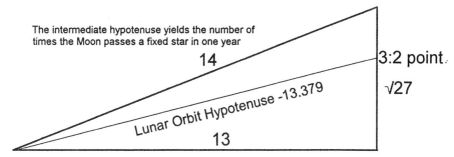

The intermediate hypotenuse yields the number of times the Moon passes a fixed star in one year

14

3:2 point.

√27

Lunar Orbit Hypotenuse -13.379

13

Figure 18. The Lunar Orbit Triangle.

So, we have found a simple geometric technique by which the other lunar time period may now be extracted using a geometric function based on right angled triangles. Both triangles offer a technique which is very precise, mathematically, geometrically, astronomically and symbolically. The lunation triangle is accurate to 0.008%, the lunar orbit triangle *to better still*. A rational technique, it requires a so-called irrational and symbolic approach to discover its secrets. The technique marries right and left brain activities, which can itself be considered a form of solar/lunar integration, and is wholly practical, having immediate applications, as the following section will amply demonstrate.

Before we develop the practical applications of these two triangles, we must look at the third one in the set, for there is yet another which carries vital information.

- The Eclipse Year Triangle -

Astronomers refer to an *'Eclipse year'* of 346.63 days in order to calculate the two 173 day periods which separate the twice yearly time when eclipses are likely to occur. This is 11.37 months, the time taken for the Sun to return to one of the Moon's nodes as it appears to journey around the zodiac. (The reason why it is less than one year is due to the fact that the nodes rotate *backwards* around the zodiac, thus a particular node meets the Sun more than once a year. The nodes rotate with a period of 18.61 years, which represents 18.61 day-degrees a year along the perimeter of the year-circle. Note also the very strange fact that 365.24 - 18.61 = 346.63 days, the Eclipse Year).[12]

This precise period may be found using a third triangle, shown below (figure 19). Here, the right angle formed by two longer sides of 11 and 12 is, once again, divided into the ratio 3:2, whence the new hypotenuse holds a length of 11.37. If the '12' side is thought to represent the solar year, with its twelve months, then the '11.37' side represents 346 days - the Eclipse Year.

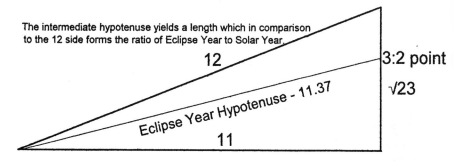

Figure 19. The 'Eclipse-year' Triangle.

We now have three triangles, which are contiguous and form part of an infinite set of right angled triangles whose design depends on whole number hypotenuses in right angled triangle whose lengths increase by unity. I have called these *N:N+1 triangles* and their design can be drawn out, whence an interesting and familiar spiral (phi-based) shape is produced (figure 20). Stonehenge is built on the remains of countless spiral shells which once housed the bodies of emerging life on this planet. It seems entirely appropriate that this triangle series links the motions of the Sun and Moon to the evolution of life on Earth and to the *'Divine Proportion'* number *phi*.

---

[12] I find the repetition of the number 18.61 astonishing, for it divides the eclipse year of 346.63 days into itself. 18.61 **days** is the square root of the eclipse year, as it is also the period in **years** of the rotation of the Moon's nodes. In the book of Ezekiel, we can read that *"I have appointed thee a day for each year"* (Ez.4.6), which neatly summarises this relationship between the eclipse year and the annual angular shift in the Moon's nodes.

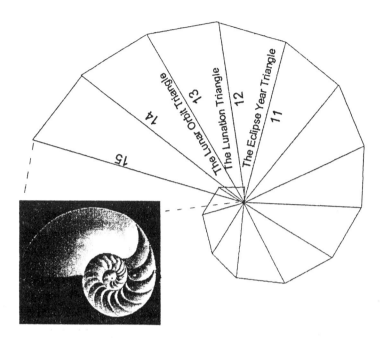

Figure 20. The Sun/Moon Triangles within their spiral family.

In the following chapter we will look at the practical outcomes which stem from knowledge of these three 'lunar' triangles. You are invited to take part in astronomical techniques which may have last taken place in megalithic Europe some 4000 or more years ago, techniques whose remnants fill our folklore, religious texts and fairy stories. These techniques are hardly vague and imprecise, for they lead to the most accurate and useful information for anyone interested in astronomy, calendars, religion, music or the evolution of life on Earth, as we shall now discover. We now are in possession of everything we need to perform some really accurate astronomy on the Sun, Moon, Earth system.

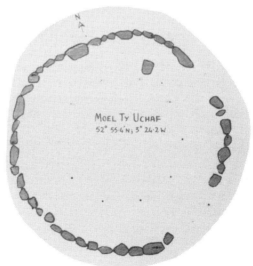

MOEL TY UCHAF
52° 55·4'N; 3° 24·2 W

Figure 21 and 22. Moel ty Uchaf: photograph and plan.

- Chapter Three -

- Practical Applications of Megalithic Designs -

Before demonstrating the following applications, it is necessary to understand the known level of technology available our ancestors during the peak period of megalith building. For example, the Aubrey and Sarsen circle must have been laid out using a rope pegged at a central point. Thus, we must conclude that the builders had access to long and, in view of the accuracy of their work, non-elastic ropes. No traces of such rope are ever likely to be found. They are thus inadmissable archaeological evidence, yet it is inconceivable that Stonehenge or any other stone ring could have been built without such equipment. The same comment applies to the many stone ellipses, egg shapes and flattened circles, each of which has a quite specific geometry - often involving right angled triangles to implement - requiring pegs and ropes.

Archaeologists are happy to concede that early man had the ability to move huge blocks of stone over long distances. There has been some success at finding our *when* stones were moved, within a few hundred years or so. They theorise, and find it perfectly acceptable to theorise, as to *how* ancient man performed such Herculean tasks. But..there are no definite answers to this question for the same reason I mention above - they cannot find any evidence as to the methods used. Yet archaeologists frequently accuse astro-archaeologists of sloppy axioms and resort to personal abuse - i.e. *The lunatic fringe of dotty archaeologists.* Meanwhile, of course, this effectively smokescreens the sad truth that they are totally unable to explain the most important question which their salary paying public requires to know: *why* were the stones moved. This text offers more than one explanation.

Whether one accepts ancient knowledge of the 'lunar triangles' with their astonishingly accurate hypotenuses, they exist as a reality and have always been available to those who strive to find order and meaning within the Cosmos. I suspect there were rather more souls within this category before our present epoch. I have shown some evidence that knowledge of the 5:12:13 triangle existed, with its lunation secret, in ancient times and across several cultures. Other megalithic sites demonstrate familiarity with the right angled triangle and with the numbers we have been dealing with. For example, the Loanhead ellipse, at Daviot and near Inverness, Scotland, contains a 5:13:14 triangle in its design - a lunar orbital triangle. Indeed, all stone ellipses use right angled triangles in their construction, many of them 'Pythagorean' (whole number ratio) or 'near-Pythagorean' ones. In Brittany, France, the alignments at Carnac contain ample evidence of sophisticated knowledge concerning right angled triangles. At Stonehenge, the number ratio 12:13 may be found to accuracies better than one quarter of one percent, as the diameter of the Aubrey circle compared with the distance from the centre of the Aubrey circle to the Heel Stone will amply testify.

Following the dedicated work of Alex Thom and others, we hold an incredible catalogue of geometrical and astronomical expertise within the corpus of known information about megalithic sites. Time and again we find that the builders were using the technology available to them in order to solve the most difficult problems concerning the relationships between the Sun, Moon and Earth. Archaeologists are beginning to incorporate some of this information within the rather conservative axioms under which they have traditionally operated. They face a very difficult situation indeed, for full acceptance of Prof. Thom's work means that the present model of European pre-history becomes almost totally bankrupt. When an engineer/scientist like Thom, who was also a first-class surveyor and astrophysicist, produces page after page of hard evidence, it is hard to maintain the *status quo* any longer, and some quite large cracks are beginning to appear in the current model. I hope that this text may accelerate an inevitable process of change.

I want to begin looking at the practical applications of megalithic architecture by taking a close look at one of the best known of the *compound rings* * - that site known as Moel ty Uchaf, near Bala in Wales. I wish to demonstrate that this site, which may be a *kerbed cairn* rather than a stone ring, has a functional value which compliments its exquisite geometry.

- *Moel Ty Uchaf* -

A photograph of the site together with a plan diagram is shown below (figures 21,22 and 23). The site commands a panoramic view extending to over 80 miles over much of the compass. The solar and lunar alignments on the horizon are evident to anyone who has visited the site armed with a theodolite and the azimuths of Sunrise and Sunset at this latitude during the year. Major and minor standstill alignments of the Moon are also present.

It is not these alignments which concern me here. The geometry of Moel ty Uchaf is beautiful, being based on a pentagonal motif. To construct the monument, the builders began with a circle of radius 7 megalithic yards, inside which they inscribed another circle of radius 4 megalithic yards. This done, they divided the perimeter of both circles by ten - a technique not thought to have

---

* The largest and most famous of the compound rings is Avebury.

pre-dated the Greeks. Presumably they placed pegs at the division points. The axis of the monument is aligned at about 18 degrees to the cardinal points of the compass, this being one quarter of 72 degrees, the pentagram angle.

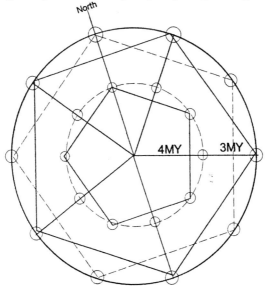

Using ropes or measuring poles, the builders then proceeded to produce the flattening effects so visible on the plan diagram. (these effects are barely noticeable on site, as the earlier photograph demonstrates). The technique is shown below (figures 22 & 23.)

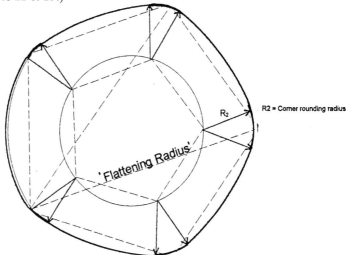

Figure 23. The Geometrical Construction of Moel ty Uchaf.

The plan of Moel ty Uchaf is very beautiful to the eye but this is hardly evident to someone viewing the site from the ground. However, it also has a very practical application for an astronomer. The perimeter of the 7 MY circle was just under 44 MY (43.98MY), whilst the perimeter of Moel ty Uchaf, as built, is 42.85MY. The ratio between these two numbers is so close (0.4%) to the ratio between lunar year (12 lunations) and the solar year that the flattening of Moel ty Uchaf holds a practical component. *If one wishes to discover when Full Moons will occur in a given year, then laying two ropes side by side - a 'year' rope (44MY) marked with the days of the year and a 'lunar year' rope (42.85MY) divided into twelve equal lengths - will indicate the exact day of Full Moon each month.* I recently took a party of about thirty people to Moel ty Uchaf and conducted an experiment. Using ordinary rope, each lunation was determined for 1993 and never more than 8 hours in error. This is better than 0.6% accuracy. Moel ty Uchaf is aesthetically superb and holds a useful practical outcome. It represents true design principles even without the astronomic component and cannot be attributed to the random strugglings of near-savages.

Now, Moel ty Uchaf is just one flattened stone ring. There are many more lying across England, Wales and Scotland. Many have degrees of flattening which make it look like their builders were attempting to make the circumference equal to 3 times the radius, rather than the irrational 'pi' (3.141592654..). If this be the case, then the builders didn't succeed very well, for their designs spill out two distinct categories of number - 3.059 and 2.957 - for 'pi'. The former number gives flattened to circle perimeter ratios like Moel ty Uchaf, which offer the lunation data, whilst the latter offers flattened to circle perimeter ratios which *directly offer the eclipse year proportioned to the solar year* - accurate to 1%. Currently, there is no official explanation as to why so many megalithic circles were flattened in such a precise way. Professor Thom recorded just how precise the flattening was, yet there are statements in archaeological journals which malign the skill of the builders by assuming that a circle was intended yet not achieved. I feel that it is an insult to the architects of these megalithic sites to assume they failed to create a circle at some sites whilst 2/3 of all stone rings are perfectly circular. A child of 9 or 10 can draw a circle using a rope pegged to an intended centre. Also, the irrational number *pi* does not present any problem when used in a purely *geometrical* context; it is only when one attempts arithmetical tasks that obstacles are placed in the way of absolute accuracy.

- Practical Applications -

- *Astronomy Using Ropes* -

Within the following applications, we shall look at just what may be achieved using the three 'lunar triangles' to develop a useful astronomy, chronology and history of the Sun, Moon, Earth system. We will discover that it is predictive. For some years I have taken student groups through the procedures to be described here, thus verifying the technique. It is, of course, left to the reader to decide whether or not these things formed part of ancient cosmology.

The technique is very simple. A lunation (or lunar orbital) triangle is constructed from rope and laid out on flat ground. The larger this is made, within limits, the better will be the accuracy of the results. The intermediate hypotenuse is found via the 3:2 point and then proportioned down to fit the 'solar year' rope, which is 12 units in length and thus supports the adoption of a 12 month year or 12 sign zodiac. The 12.369 (or 13.379) length of the hypotenuse is 'fitted' within the same length as the 365.24 day 'solar year' rope. Evidence of neolithic ability to proportion triangles is readily found at many sites. Carnac is perhaps the most spectacular display of such talents, and clearly this technique was known about and used by neolithic and bronze age astronomers.

Below is an example of the process using the 5:12:13 lunation triangle. Figure 24(a) shows the constructed lunation hypotenuse, which is pivoted from the apex of the triangle and brought down adjacent to the '12' side, whose twelve divisions are transferred across.

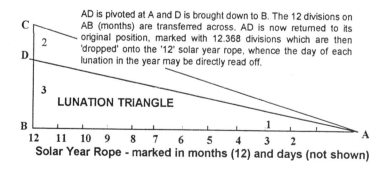

Figure 24. Proportioning the Lunation hypotenuse into the Solar Year

The hypotenuse is thus marked with 12.369 divisions; these now needing to be proportionately reduced in spacing to 'fit' the '12' rope, which represents the year. Figure 24(b) illustrates one simple geometric technique - the resulting 'lunation rope' can then be used to indicate the date of every Full Moon during the course of the current year. Folding the rope between each Full Moon will then deliver New Moon dates (fold once) and the dates of the quarter Moons (fold twice).

Ten and eleven year old children were able to calculate every Full Moon during 1993 to the day using a 50 metre lunation triangle

If many solar year ropes are laid end to end, and multiple lunation ropes are made to lie adjacent and parallel to them starting at a known Full or New Moon date (an eclipse would be the ideal starting point), then all subsequent or past lunations may be accurately dated. Just like the old slide rule, the dates may be read off directly[13] . The accuracy with a 200 metre year rope is such that the exact time of the lunation during one day/night period may be seen - often to better than an hour.

Of course, the same technique may also be applied to the lunar orbit triangle in order to establish the position of the Moon with respect to the fixed stars for a given day; in other words, to establish the zodiacal position of the Moon. Accuracy better than five degrees, two years in the future is possible. It is worth mentioning two important factors at this juncture: the first is that the lunation period of 29.53059 days is an average figure, the moment of lunation can vary by a total of *thirteen* hours from this figure - plus or minus 6.5 hours. The

---

[13] If you don't know what a slide rule is, ask an engineer over 40 years old. Or maybe over 4000 years old.

second factor is that the 56 hole Aubrey calendar could only offer, at best, a resolution of half a day. The Station Stone rectangle, with its 5:12:13 application, offers a vast improvement. Perhaps this is why it was built just some few hundred years after the Aubrey holes - a 'Mark Two'. In modern advertising terms, the builders slapped a 'New! Improved!' label on Stonehenge.

The secret of accuracy, based on my own experience, lies in the ability to pull both ropes with equal force. Apart from this, dampness and other environmental factors do not affect results, providing the ropes share the same environment. Proportional methods always offer this advantage, and rope astronomy, using materials, techniques and dimensions known to have been prevalent at neolithic sites produces highly accurate results with ease.

- Eclipse Prediction -

To predict eclipses requires knowledge of the 346 day 'Eclipse Year'. Although we have (re)discovered a triangle which offers this period as a length correctly proportioned to the solar year, the same ratio may be found elsewhere at Stonehenge. When discussing the Sarsen Circle, the perimeter turned out to be 3652 primitive inches in length. This is ten times the solar year in the same units. Now, the Aubrey Circle diameter is 3459 of those self-same units. Thus, even without using the eclipse year triangle, the relevent ratio may be found at Stonehenge to an accuracy of better than 0.1%. In other words:-

> **The ratio between the Aubrey circle diameter and the perimeter of the Sarsen circle is the same as that between the eclipse year (346 days) and the solar year (365.24 days).**

To predict eclipses requires that the '11.37' hypotenuse is used with the '12' solar year rope and the lunation rope. Like the Greenwich 'pips' used to reset a watch, one begins the eclipse prediction process by laying the eclipse year rope with its end lying adjacent to the date on the solar rope where an eclipse was known to have occured.

Because there are two 'eclipse seasons' in the year, the eclipse year rope must be marked halfway - by folding it in two. This mark, and the other end of the eclipse year rope, then indicates the next two 'eclipse seasons', dates when solar or lunar eclipses *may* occur. However, the lunation rope will rarely indicate a Full or New Moon coincident with this precise day. Depending on how far away the nearest lunation (Full or New Moon) lies from the eclipse year rope markers will determine the degree of totality of any eclipse. If exact, a total eclipse may be expected. Up to 17 days away, the eclipse will be less and less exact until the current cycle of eclipses is broken, whence there is a gap of *thirteen* months before the next cycle commences. If a lunar eclipse occurs during the day, it, too, will not be visible at the site. Lunar eclipses are capricious although regular events at any given location, total solar eclipses almost never occur at the latitude of Stonehenge.

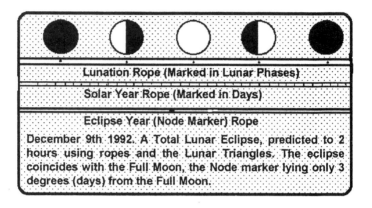

Figure 25. Eclipse predicting using ropes.

Using rope techniques with a student group in 1990, the accuracy obtained was such that the total lunar eclipse on December 9th 1992 was predictable to within 6 hours, certainly adequate to establish that it would be visible (during the night) at Stonehenge.

Thus the three lunar triangles would have allowed, then as now, an astronomer to perform the necessary duties required by the society in order to structure time and to predict phenomena relating to the Sun and Moon. All these things can be achieved using rope and simple geometry, this begging an important question. No ropes are ever going to be found at Stonehenge - they are long since rotted away - yet we know, from reconstructions of Bronze and Iron Age huts, that long lengths of leather and fibre ropes were available. Do we continue to deny important evidence about megalithic sites because the stones have endured whilst the rope has rotted? Another question: How was continuity of observational techniques carried on for over a millenium at Stonehenge? In other words, how was the data stored? Stored it certainly must have been, orally transmitting or receiving the last few thousand lunations is somewhat unrealistic a task even if we are to believe the prodigious memory feats achieved within the colleges of the Druids! Knowledge of these three triangles provides a superb 'shorthand' method for *deriving* the information; rope lengths for *storing* the information.

The so-called *cursus* which lies just to the north of Stonehenge has never been adequately explained, yet it would form an ideal site for the rope astronomy and calendar techniques described above. After several attempts, my college students decided that an airfield runway or a beach would form the best site. Fortunately, we had access to both and doesn't the cursus look *so much* like a runway (figure 26)?

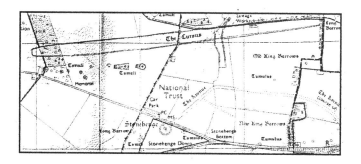

Figure 26. The Cursus at Stonehenge.

- *Tidal Prediction* -

The Aubrey Calendar can also be used to furnish a delightfully simple tidal predictor. Here, it finds a role more as a clock. A full description of how to use the Aubrey calendar may be found earlier (figure 8). To adapt it for tidal use requires that one constructs a 24 hour circular clock to fit concentrically within the 56 markers. Mark a horizontal 'local horizon' between 6 am and 6 pm.

Local high tide always occurs when the Moon is in the same two relative positions in the sky. If you live near the sea you may check this statement, if not, then you will have to trust my word for it. Don't ask a fisherman! Most appear to have lost this important piece of knowledge by which you can estimate the tides. Once you have ascertained for your locality just where the Moon is located in the sky at high tide, then mark it on the perimeter of the 24 hour clock face relative to the local horizon line. Place an identical marker opposite it, and two 'low tide' markers perpendicular to both. The finished model is shown in figure 27.

To operate the clock, simply point either 'high tide' marker at the currently held position of the Moon marker on the outer perimeter of the Aubrey calendar. A line from the centre of the Aubrey calendar - the Earth and 24-hour clock - to the current Sun marker will indicate the time of high tide, for the given location.

You can find low tides and the other high tide in the same way, using the other three markers.

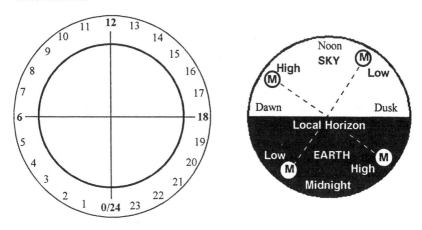

Figure 27. Tidal 'clock' for use with Aubrey Calendar.

I have found this technique to be accurate to within an hour and usually to within a half hour, making tide tables somewhat superfluous. It is important to recognise that weather conditions can alter the range and times of tides by much more than half an hour. The highest tides of the month occur two days after Full and New Moon, the lowest tides two days after the quarter Moons. The Aubrey clock/calendar will show these dates exactly. The highest tides of the year often occur at the lunations which align with the current nodal marker positions, although the Moon's 14 month *apogee* and *perigee* rhythm adds a further dimension to tidal prediction. However, eclipses and very high tides are linked.

- Menstrual calendar -

The Aubrey calendar may be used to assist in keeping records of menstruation and ovulation, something which both women and men need to understand if they are to optimise harmony within their relationship and family. The menstrual cycle normally follows the lunation cycle. It is not often very constant, although using the Aubrey calendar to mark these events is certainly much clearer and more sensible than trying to shove a cyclic event place into the totally unsuitable square format of the average kitchen calendar.

Each month it becomes possible to see how constant the cycle is, and whether 'advanced' or 'retarded' in its normal duration. Like a clock which runs fast or slow, the current month's markers will assist in a better understanding of this important cyclic process in a woman's metabolism.

- *Use in Skywatching* -

Using the 24 hour clock feature, the Aubrey calendar may be used to navigate around the night sky. A central circle within the clock is divided into two halves; the half between 6 pm and 6 am (below the horizon) is shaded black whilst the other half is left white. Rotating the clock until the current time points at the Sun marker will then indicate, approximately, that half of the sky which is visible above the horizon - the white half of the 24-hour clock circle shows which constellations will be visible. The dividing line between the black and white half represents the local horizon.

Allowance must be made for summer time and this technique is not very accurate within a month either side of the solstices, where it may be 'out' by thirty degrees. However, it gives a good guide as to which stars and planets will be visible on a given night and performs very well indeed within the tropics. A model of the Aubrey calendar must have the principle visible stars drawn on its outer perimeter.

If you wish to adapt this idea to suit astrological purposes, then bear in mind that most astrologers and nearly all astrology books use the tropical zodiac, which is currently 25 degrees behind the sidereal zodiac (where the actual constellations are in the sky). If a tropical zodiac is marked on the outer perimeter of the Aubrey markers, then it is possible to place natal positions of the planets in their correct positions. Current transits may then be placed. The writer accepts no responsibility for what you may predict from such experimentation!

The above practical uses for the Aubrey calendar and lunar triangles form an interesting and instructive way by which one may reconnect to the rhythms which surround and engulf the planet. With the details supplied here, it should be possible for any moderately practical soul to construct accurate working models of the Sun, Moon, Earth system. Already, I know of several large 'sidereal lawn clocks' based on the Aubrey Circle, all fully operational and all accurately showing the season, the age of the Moon, the phase of the Moon and other matters relating to eclipses, tides, solstices and equinoxes. Of course, what is needed is for the existing full size model to be restored and operated at Stonehenge. Failing this, surely there must be room for a replica within the grounds of the proposed new 'Stonehenge Centre'? I have shown that, quite apart from its neolithic pedigree, it provides an exceptional educational aid to understanding the apparently complex motions of the Sun and the Moon* .

---

* Readers wishing to construct a 56 marker Aubrey calendar may obtain an A3 sized template and a DIY booklet. For details and current prices, send a stamped addressed envelope to the publishers at the address given on the inside front cover.

The view looking south from the Preseli Bluestone site at *Carn Menyn*. The horizon shows the *Cleddau* estuary, near Milford Haven, and the river *Cleddau* has one source within a mile or so of this site, raising the question as to whether or not the stones - some of which weighed over 4 tons - were floated to the sea and then taken up the Bristol Channel. On a clear day, Caldey island, near Tenby, can be seen. The top of the Preseli mountains are littered with important megalithic sites, many unexplored.

- *Chapter Four* -

- Stonehenge and Ancient Cosmology -

So far, I have described a coherent and integrated explanation for the inevitable design and form which the earlier phases of Stonehenge had to take in order to accurately plot the rhythms of the Sun and Moon. In addition, I have demonstrated some geometric techniques which allow both integration and increased accuracy within these rhythms, these techniques offering an immediate practical application, enabling accurate forecasting of lunations, lunar position and eclipses.

I hope that I have shown that every technological aid for implementing these highly accurate techniques was to be found at Stonehenge. Archaeologically, the only missing hardware is the ropes themselves, although evidence of their use in laying out the various circular forms at Stonehenge is obvious. The passage of the years has eradicated all evidence of these ropes and although the evidence for an ancient knowledge of the lunar triangles exists, it survives through forms not directly connected with ropes nor the neolithic period. Babylonian clay tablets and Egyptian Heiroglyphs have fared rather better in this respect. Perhaps our current perspective concerning the growth of civilisation and scientific endeavour is wrongly slanted towards the Middle East because of the simple fact that rope, as a vehicle to convey and *store* information, decays quite quickly whilst clay tablets and carved stones do not.

Whether or not our European ancestors conceived of Stonehenge with or without cultural assistance from other lands is something the reader must decide from the evidence presented here, and in other books. If they did not, then the current model of this period of history must be redefined, away from the 'woad covered savages' theme beloved of many historians. However, if these folk received assistance from any other culture then the implications are perhaps even more profound. Both you cannot have; if you take the *separate culture* model, then questions like 'why does the Sarsen circle have a circumference which relates to the Aubrey Circle diameter to form a ratio which is equal to the solar year/eclipse year ratio?' and 'Why is Stonehenge so beautifully sited, to allow the impressive display of 5:12:13 geomantics across southern Britain?' and 'Why does the Aubrey Circle provide the only sensible way of producing a model of the Sun, Moon, Earth system on the ground, which must use 56 holes?' have to be answered.

If you adopt the alternative *cultural interchange* model, then which way must interchange have flowed? Could it have been two-way? Why are factors related to Stonehenge to be found within the corpus of Christian and Jewish literature and within Egyptian pyramids? Why does the Sarsen circle perimeter replicate the Egyptian quarter *Aroura*? Instead of mocking the outcomes of astro-archaeological work, perhaps archaeologists should be facing these questions squarely and honestly as the primary questions worth answering about Stonehenge.

Whilst the earlier chapters of this book dealt with aspects of Stonehenge which may be verified by anyone prepared to take the trouble, I felt that in order to complete the message I wish to convey, it was necessary to include an additional chapter which highlights some of the less objective and more conjectural aspects of Stonehenge which were thrown up by my researches.

-From Archaeology to Cosmology -

We have discovered that Stonehenge is a highly practical monument reflecting the eternal rounds of the Sun and Moon. I believe that these practical aspects have never been properly expounded by archaeologists or historians, perhaps because their implications for the current model of world history would be professionally ruinous, making them appear foolish. Indeed, the leading works during the past few decades, concerning the function of Stonehenge, have come not from archaeologists nor historians but from scientists and engineers (Sir Fred Hoyle, Prof. Alex Thom, Dr Gerald Hawkins and Dr John Wood.)

Archaeologists, like the late Professor Richard Atkinson and Dr Aubrey Burl, have provided a different sort of information about Stonehenge. Burl's *The Stonehenge People* is a fascinating and well written book, offering exhaustive information concerning the social and medical histories of people who lived and died around the monument; information derived primarily from the exhumation of burial chambers. As a consequence of this, Dr Burl sees Stonehenge - not surprisingly, perhaps - as an impressive charnelhouse and he *protesteth too much* concerning the lack of mathematical and logical reasoning evidenced by Neolithic and Bronze Age folk.

On his criteria and with his axioms, this is an inevitable result although he does bring a valuable contribution to our knowledge of these distant times. However, it must be clear from this text (and some others) that at least some members of the local neolithic populace demonstrated a rather more advanced knowledge of astronomy, geometry and mathematics than Dr Burl was able to find within tombs. One would not look in graveyards to understand the twentieth century. Perhaps we need to learn that cultural messages can be just as plainly understood from the geometry, siting and numerical relationships of Stonehenge as they can from jewellery, pottery shards, bones and flint arrowheads. Certainly, all the main astronomical constants of the Sun, Moon and Earth may be read from the monument. And if *God is a geometer* then studying the geometry of the natural universe, including early man's attempts to understand it through the motions of the two 'lights' or luminaries, would be one valid way of understanding God and hence the creation or evolution of life on Earth. This has been the surprising message from my researches into Stonehenge and megalithic thought, although it was not at all an expected outcome.

I believe that with the (re)discovery of the 'lunar triangles' and their scientific and practical cargo of hypotenuses, which connect **all** the inter-relationships of the Sun, Moon and Earth in their correct ratios, we are in possession of a new key by which we can unlock more of the secrets of Stonehenge. The lunation triangle may be found quite precisely described within the modern Bible, another example appears to form part of a 'Stonehenge complex', laid out quite precisely across southern Britain. References to the lunation and lunar orbital triangle may be discovered in the placement of the King's and Queen's chamber in the Great Pyramid. These triangles yield astronomic constants, beyond opinion, and they form a scientifically valid and astonishingly accurate model of the way by which the orbit of Moon interacts with the Earth's orbit around the Sun. Stonehenge reflects and supports this model and archaeology would do well to investigate *why* ancient man was so taken up with measurements of the two Luminaries.

If one wishes to understand the mind of megalithic man, then Stonehenge is where one naturally begins. If one wishes to discover the cosmology lying behind Stonehenge, then the ancient world already tells the would be initiate that *God is a geometer* and to look to simple geometry, the golden section number, *phi* and right-angle triangles. The greatest astronomer of the renaissance of modern science, Johannes Kepler (1571-1630), even went as far as to state just that.

> *Geometry has two treasures; one is the theorem of Pythagoras;*
> *the other, the division of a line into extreme and mean ratio (the*
> *golden section). The first we may compare to a measure of gold;*
> *the second we may name a precious jewel.*

It is strange that neither *treasure* may be seen within Kepler's three planetary laws, yet both pour out from the stones of megalithic monuments. The three lunar triangles re-discovered here lead into a better model of the Sun, Moon, Earth system. We have seen how the design of Stonehenge leads to a better calendar structure and to simple practical solutions to lunation, eclipse, tidal and other lunar related problems. In our rush as a species to become ever more secure in an apparently insecure universe and ever more in control of the environment - a domination goal which this century has become visibly and severely flawed - we have taken some wrong turnings and forgotten some of the essential rules about living   harmoniously   on   the   Earth.   This   book   reflects something of what these rules or laws might have been from what I have gleaned from the builders of Stonehenge. Approaching the geometry and astronomy of Stonehenge as a scientist/engineer, I have reported here just what I found, however misaligned this appears to current archaeological or cosmological fashion.

To challenge contemporary western thinking has become impossible through the professional journals associated with each specific subject field. Even the more popular magazines, such as *Nature* and *New Scientist*, refuse to consider any material which aims the axe too near the bole of the belief tree we have zealously guarded and watered over the last couple of millenia. Also, the reader should understand that most specialisms are so focussed as to prevent their experts and specialists looking further afield. Knowledge has become dangerously pigeon-holed so that cross-disciplinary research is rather rare.

One of the grosser assumptions made by our culture is that science - specifically the science of astronomy - was conceived in Babylon, refined in Egypt and presented 'scientifically' in Greece. The neolithic culture is either ignored or taken to be wholly independent, even though it predates Egypt and Greek culture. Because the approach taken in this book embraces several specialisms, I want to now take a spectacular example which shows how mixing astronomy, archaeology, religious history and megalithic monuments delivers a fatal blow to this assumption.

- Enoch's Portals -

The Book of Enoch used to be found within the Old Testament of every Bible. It was removed during one of the revisionist periods which led to the King James' version yet may still be found in some of the many translations of the old testament and is freely available as a separate book from SPCK, London.

There are two quite distinct versions of Enoch, the first is a pre-Christian text called *1 Enoch* or *Ethiopian Enoch* to distinguish it from the later *2 Enoch* or *Slavonic Enoch*, discovered in Yugoslavia in 1886 and which is thought to be contemporary with the Christian era. The former text contains a calendar which is 364 day based, the latter a 365 day calendar. *1 Enoch*, originally an aramaic text is filled with references to factors 2, 4, 7, 14, 28, 91 and 364, whilst *2 Enoch* dishes up the Roman Calendar. Both versions drop the 13 month factor and adopt a 12 month format, although the authors or revisionists of *1 Enoch* appear to be struggling hard at times to comply with this bizarre move within factors which so suit a 13 month year. By the time *2 Enoch* was written, its Greek editor presumably knew which side his bread was buttered on and aligned the text with Roman calendrical fashion.

The whole structure and subsequent history of the Western Christian era is based on foundations which are rooted in the New Testament of the Bible - the Christian story. Whether you believe this story or not is irrelevent here; what is important is to recognise that religious historians attribute much of the material in the New Testament to Enoch, i.e. *to a text written before the alleged time of Jesus*. Within the Jewish heirarchy, Enoch is one of the major prophets, ranking alongside Moses, Abraham, Isaac, Jacob, Elijah.

The assumption made is that Enoch belongs to the Middle Eastern cultural tradition, yet it is stated within *1 Enoch* that *"from thence I went towards the north to the ends of the Earth, and there I saw a great and glorious device."* Hmm! Furthermore, we can read, *"And I saw in those days how long cords were given to those angels, and they took themselves wings and flew, and they went towards the north. And I asked the angel, saying unto him: "Why have those angels taken these cords and gone off?" And he said to me: "They have gone off to measure"."*

This is reasonably specific information about a northern *glorious device* where measurements were being taken using long cords. I am sure the reader can understand my interest in Enoch just on this basis, but there is much more specific information to link, if not the monument, then the latitude at which Stonehenge is found.

In Chapter LXXII, *The Book of the Courses of the Heavenly Luminaries*, the angel Uriel helpfully and accurately describes to Enoch a complete annual cycle of solar and lunar observations within a portal based structure which is implied as being circular in shape. Astronomically, the text is accurate, and the Sun and Moon are described as rising within six portals in the east and setting within six portals in the west. (There are also many 'windows' to the right and left of these portals.) For each month following the spring equinox, Enoch tells the reader in which portal the Sun rises and sets and, more importantly for this text, he tells us **the specific ratio of day to night lengths during the first day of that month.** Because the cycle of the Sun's risings and settings is sinusoidal, each number sequence is repeated four times, so we can be assured of no errors of translation. Using a simple computer program available to every secondary school, it is possible to work a little astrophysics on *1 Enoch. Because day/night ratios vary according to latitude, we can determine at what latitude Enoch took his observations.*

It does appear that Enoch's observations were taken at or very near the latitude of Stonehenge, as the graph below ably demonstrates. The day/night ratio gradient is the same as for Stonehenge, and if the definition of 'night' was taken to be half an hour different from sunrise/set, such as the time the first stars became visible, then the graph for Enoch's observations and for Stonehenge would coincide.

So, Enoch's writings, long assumed to contain only Jewish and/or Middle-Eastern wisdom, contain an influence from *a great and glorious device* found *very* near to the latitude of Stonehenge and from which very accurate and specific astronomical information was observed and recorded using a 364 day calendar structure. Such coincidences begin to look rather like evidence for cultural interchange, don't they, and Stonehenge is in Britain, not Syria or Lebanon?

For the Sun to rise and set within six portals on each side of an observer at Stonehenge, one can deduce that Enoch must have taken his observations within the Sarsen circle at the location now referred to as *The Grave* - the entrance to the elliptical or horse-shoe shaped set of five trilithons within the Sarsen circle. This is a most auspicious and appropriate place at Stonehenge from which to observe and I conclude that the text of *1 Enoch* contains enough evidence to link the prophet to the monument.

No-one knows who the authors of this fascinating collection of ancient material were. Astonishingly, in our Celtic heritage, we find in *The Tales of Taliesin*, "*I was instructor to Eli and Enoch*". Robert Graves* was quick to point out the apparent absurdity of Gwion, the celtic writer, understanding Ethiopian, the language of the only known extant text of *1 Enoch*. Whoever or whatever Enoch represented we can be sure that his mention within some of the oldest surviving Celtic literature - the *Mabinogion* - links British folklore with the prophet. Even within a few miles of the Preseli Bluestone site one can find *Carn Enoch*, and the root word *cnoc* is thought to mean carved stone or ceremonial stone.

Finally, we may add that Enoch telling us "*And the course of the path of the Moon is light to the righteous*" ** is a most odd remark for an alleged paid-up member of the Patriarchy to make - it is bizarre within a Judao-Christian context. Anyone who has studied megalithic lunar observatories in Northern Europe will recognise their builder's total pre-occupation with understanding just that - *the course of the path of the Moon.* Enoch's phrase has no place nor cultural connection with traditional Jewish or Christian philosophic roots. Perhaps the reader can see that here I have presented material which needs to be urgently considered within any revision of history.

---

* *The White Goddess*, p 193.
** Chapter XLI. 3 - 9; *Astronomic Secrets*.

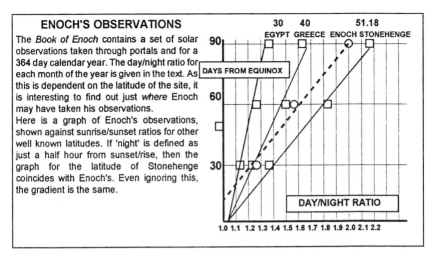

ENOCH'S OBSERVATIONS

The *Book of Enoch* contains a set of solar observations taken through portals and for a 364 day calendar year. The day/night ratio for each month of the year is given in the text. As this is dependent on the latitude of the site, it is interesting to find out just *where* Enoch may have taken his observations.

Here is a graph of Enoch's observations, shown against sunrise/sunset ratios for other well known latitudes. If 'night' is defined as just a half hour from sunset/rise, then the graph for the latitude of Stonehenge coincides with Enoch's. Even ignoring this, the gradient is the same.

- *Stonehenge - What Next?* -

There is another side to Stonehenge, a facet of the monument and its siting which cannot be treated in quite the same objective and practical manner as the laws implied above. One could call this the monument's *mystical* side, in the sense that one cannot fully explain many of the properties which follow through the scientific method alone - at least, *not yet.* Within the next few pages may be found some other strange and fascinating aspects of this 'other side'; aspects with which any researcher will inevitably have to meet, work with and, ultimately, understand.

A woman once asked Sir Michael Faraday, "What use is your electric motor?", to which he replied, curtly, "Madam, what use is a new-born baby?" I believe that we are in the same position with much of the information to which we now turn.

- *Stonehenge and the Pyramids* -

Although it may seem preposterous, it is an easy task to demonstrate that there are strong links between these two most famous sites. Furthermore, these links are inextricably connected with the 5:12:13 triangle - the lunation triangle.

A *Great Circle* is a circle which passes over the surface of the planet and which shares the same centre. By and large, satellites orbit in great circle orbits (or ellipses) and navigation by great circle offers ships and aircraft the shortest distances between two ports of call. The section of the great circle which connects Stonehenge and the Great Pyramid has some very interesting properties. The first of these is that it leaves the Giza complex heading at an angle of about 50.4° north of west. This angle, which is about a seventh of a circle, also approximates to the base angle of the Pyramid (51.85°). It is also the approximate latitude of Stonehenge (51.17°) as it is the approximate angle of the midsummer sunrise azimuth at Stonehenge (51.25°).

> **Stonehenge is thus uniquely although approximately placed at the intersection of all these angles each of which is one seventh of a circle.**

If we continue the arc of this great circle beyond Stonehenge, we discover that it passes **within a mile or two of the Preseli bluestone site.** The lack of precision is my own, I cannot find a spherical geometry navigational program which takes account of the bulging of the Earth near the equator. (At least two international airlines inform me that they assume a truly spherical shape within their computer programs on aircraft.) After travelling over 2000 miles from Egypt, we are close enough to the Preseli site for my point to be valid.

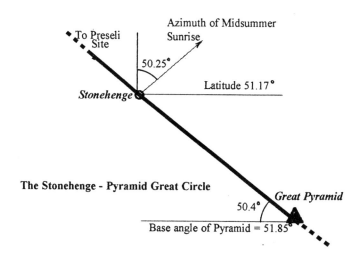

Figure 28. The Giza-Stonehenge Great Circle.

> **Between Stonehenge and the Preseli site, a great circle shares the same hypotenuse as the giant 5:12:13 triangle connecting Lundy Island, Caldey Island, the Preseli site and Stonehenge.**

This is a remarkable statement, for once again we discover the unique siting of Stonehenge. We can also state, whatever it may ultimately mean:-

> The great circle which connects the Great Pyramid to Stonehenge and the Preseli bluestone site aligns with the hypotenuse of the 5:12:13 lunation triangle. This great circle can only offer the opportunity for such a geometric event at four places of about 200 miles in length around the 24,000 mile journey it makes whilst encircling the Earth.

Although we again face the fact that this great circle is not a physical feature to be investigated or probed by archaeological methods, it does surround itself with some pretty impressive geometry. It offers another reason for the choice of siting for Stonehenge. Also, the great circle passes through other sacred sites at Mecca, Crete, Western Greece and Ireland.

There is one more curiosity which came out of my work with great circles and spherical geometry: it appears that this particular great circle runs over the least land mass possible for any great circle which runs through both Egypt and Stonehenge. (Contrast this statement with the fact that the north-south meridian through the Great Pyramid tracks along the longest north-south land mass to be found anywhere on the globe.)

- Stonehenge and Ley-lines -

The large 5:12:13 triangle found between Stonehenge and the Preseli site mimics that found within the Station Stone rectangle. If we then postulate the existence of a huge 5:12 rectangle in southern Britain to match, then it would not be too surprising to discover the thickest concentration of important neolithic sites lying on such a rectangle. Indeed, this is the case; Avebury, Cleeve Hill and Trecastell Ring are some of the better known ones; there are scores more. The Rollright Stones lie a little way off the rectangle, but on exactly the same latitude as the Preseli site. Whilst I determined not to mention the word 'ley-line' within this text, the reader will understand that the huge 5:12:13 triangle coupled with the impressive collection of sites, intelligently placed, which lie on the associated 5:12 rectangle, comes remarkably close to Alfred Watkin's original definition of a ley-line*.

---

* *The Old Straight Track.* Alfred Watkins. First published in 1925 by Methuen and has been infuriating archaeologists ever since.

- *Stonehenge and Sacred Geometry* -

Most of the discoveries contained here contain the most fundamental references to what is termed 'Sacred Geometry'. The rhythms and cycles of the Sun and Moon produce an exquisite geometry to those initiated into comprehending it. Evolution depends on and has developed from these cycles.

So far, at Stonehenge, we have concerned ourselves with the shorter cycles within the Sun, Moon, Earth system. There are longer ones, and now we must turn our attention to the most well known of these.

- *The Precessional Cycle* -

The precessional cycle occurs as a further consequence of the Earth's axial tilt (currently 23.5°). On an annual basis, this tilt produces the seasons and is thus responsible for all the yearly travellings of the Sun and the Moon along the horizon. Longer term, this angular displacement produces the precessional cycle whereby the fixed stars in the zodiac appear to rotate backwards around the seasons with a period of about 26,000 years; the longest cycle connected with the Sun, Moon, Earth system. Every 2166 years (approximately) the Sun rises in a different zodiacal sign at the spring equinox. Currently, it rises in the sign Pisces, although we are coming to the end of the 'Age of Pisces' and it will, during the next two centuries, rise in the last degree of the sign Aquarius. The long and prematurely heralded 'Age of Aquarius' will finally have arrived.

The Piscean age began, 2000 years ago, with the Christian story. The fish motif is obvious to anyone within this story; less obvious perhaps is the Piscean theme of sacrifice and confusion. Unless you hold a smattering of astrological knowledge, it is difficult to understand that 'Christ, born of a virgin' may have something to do with the opposite sign, Virgo. There is considerable evidence that Jesus was born in September, during 7 bc. Certainly, he was not born in 0 bc, for King Herod died some years previously and presumably could not have ordered the death of male infants after his own demise. The birth of Jesus is currently tagged onto the older pagan festival of the midwinter solstice, a festival saturated in symbols relating to the death of the old king (the Sun of the waning year) and the birth of the new king (the waxing Sun of the new year). This is entirely appropriate a symbol of the original Christian message - one *Age* giving way to the next.

It is instructive to look at the current meanings attributed to each sign of the zodiac during their span through history. The *Taurean Age* produced the massive and enduring stone monument building so typical of a 'fixed earth' sign. Bull motifs ran throughout human mythology. The *Arien Age* followed, with emphasis on the production of an iron based weaponry, war and the emphasis on masculine values so typical of the Patriarchs, who took over control at the commencement of the age. Aries is depicted by the ram - the Jewish tribes were known as *The Ram* or *The Horns of the Ram* in ancient texts. Jewish rules forbad the presence of women in many situations and the battle call for the tribes was to be sounded through '*the horn of a ram*'. Abraham's conflict concerning the earlier ages' demand for human sacrifices was solved through him removing the ram caught 'in a thicket' and substituting the beast for his own son, Isaac. We still use the term *battering ram* to describe the unchecked energy of this Mars ruled fire sign. The metal iron is attributed to Mars, the 'ruler' of Aries and the Iron Age coincided with the beginning of the *Age of Aries*. Bronze is fashioned from copper, the preceding Bronze Age began under the *Age of Taurus*; Taurus is ruled by Venus, whose attributed metal is copper. And so we can go on, finding correlations between astrological lore and historical events.

The precessional cycle appears to have been known by the architect of the Great Pyramid and a study of the base foundations of this monument yields further information about Stonehenge. The base perimeter of the Great Pyramid is 36,524 primitive inches around. This once again makes an arithmetical statement about the solar year. The sum of the two diagonals across the base square measure 25,827 primitive inches - a figure within half a percent of the somewhat variable precessional 'year'. Furthermore, the Pyramid's design is based on two circles, one having a circumference of 36,524 inches; the other 25,827 inches. These two numbers interplay within the entire design of the Pyramid, often with dividers or multipliers of 10, 100 or 1000, and it is interesting to discover that the relationship between the Earth's orbital period and the precessional period, 365.242 : 25,827 is a function of the square root of 2 - that 'difficult' irrational number avoided, wherever possible, by the Pythagoreans.

The base square of the Pyramid thus has a single diagonal length of 12,928 inches, which is remarkably close to 13,000, a multiple of the Aubrey circle diameter, this number being implied through the 5:12:13 triangle it contains.

We have already seen the emergence of the Golden Section number, *phi*, within our researches on Stonehenge. Any sacred geometry text will also throw up this ubiquitous and irrational number of evolution. Modern sacred geometers, at least from Greek times, seem to have disassociated themselves from the link connecting geometry and its roots within the cosmos, this too easily making the subject an abstraction. This trend has been counteracted by the work of Rudolph Steiner, Buckmeister Fuller, Chris Day and other architects, designers and innovators in this century. Steiner in particular strove to restore our links to the cosmos within geometry.

Stonehenge is sited at a latitude where, viewed from the Earth's axis, all the various concentric circles which form phases I through to III(c) take on the shape of a 'Golden Ellipse', i.e. an ellipse whose major to minor axis ratio is in the ratio *phi:1*. Thus, once again, we find the monument uniquely sited at the only latitude where this phi relationship can occur. However, we can connect sacred geometry with *phi* and Stonehenge much more closely than this, taking in the Sun/Moon/Earth system and a most ancient occult or esoteric symbol as we do so.

- *The Lunation Pentagram* -

The pentagram star contains more *phi* ratios than any other known shape, in addition to being the quintessential expression of fiveness. Strange things happen when one inscribes a pentagram star within the Aubrey circle is shown in figure 29. The length of one of the 'star' arms becomes 12.364, a length within 0.04% of the lunation period (12.368).

> A pentagram star inscribed within the Aubrey circle offers directly the $\sqrt{153}$ length needed to perform all the lunation measurements covered earlier, if and only if the Aubrey circle diameter is taken to be 13 units.

If we look at the entire perimeter of the 'star' we discover its length is five times 12.364, a figure which is 61.82 - or 100 times *phi'*. And the reader is forced to face the fact that the number of lunations in the year is directly related to the *Divine Proportion*. Does this explain something of the enduring nature of the pentagram star throughout history, as a carrier of sacred esoteric information about the realities of life on Earth?

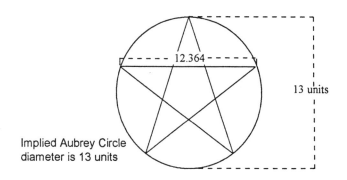

Figure 29. The Lunation Pentagram

These are very interesting relationships. The pentagon and its associated pentagram (the star shape) are very ancient magical symbols indeed. In modern times, the shape is almost inevitably wheeled out during every corny horror film when the director wants to create the atmosphere of superstition, hidden forces, the supernatural or an act of witch-craft or magic. Now we are finding a practical application for this beautiful geometric shape - it provides astronomical data relating to the Sun, Moon, Earth system. Does it offer anything else?

One of the oldest creation stories in the world, the *Enuma Elish*, came from the Sumerian civilisation which ultimately gave way to the present Patriarchal world order. The story, perhaps originating from the third millenium bc, was 'adapted' by the Patriarchs and may be found, almost intact and with the predictable exclusion clauses for the Moon, in the very first chapter of the best selling book in the world - the Bible. Here, In Genesis, Chapter One, the seven days of creation follow a specific order where each day is represented by one of the seven visible planets. Mythologically, it is easy to relate each planet to each day of creation, this fact still evident by the fact that each of the days of the week are named after a planet. The table illustrates the point clearly,

The Genesis Creation Story with its Planetary Symbolism

The Planetary order and Mythological basis for Creation		
Day	Planet	Correlation with Genesis Creation Story
Sunday	Sun	Light
Monday	Moon	Division of the Waters (tides)
Tuesday	Mars	Dry Land/Trees
Wednesday	Mercury	Seasons/Astronomy
Thursday	Jupiter	Sea Beasts/Birds
Friday	Venus	Evolution, Reproduction
Saturday	Saturn	Repose

An observant soul may well ask why the order of the days of the week is 'pied' or scrambled away from any simple astronomical arrangement. Here, we can find some intelligent cosmology, hidden somewhat from view and yet delightfully explicit once understood. It concerns the pentagram once more. The order of the visible planets (*excluding the Sun and Moon*) follows the orbital distances of each: - Mercury, Venus, Mars, Jupiter and Saturn. Placed in this order around the points of a pentagon, one can readily transduce the order to that found in the creation story. A pentagram can be drawn with just five strokes of the pen - try drawing one within the same pentagon, and, beginning at Mars

(Tuesday), make five strokes and watch how the pen traces out the days of the week/days of creation from Tuesday to Saturday; Mars, Mercury, Jupiter, Venus and Saturn (See figure 30).

The Babylonian creation story thus has encrypted within itself knowledge about the orbital distances and hence angular speeds of the planets via the order of the days of the week as expressed through this simple geometrical function (figure 30).

This function is neat and elegant, once more stressing the pentagram as an important cosmological symbol. But what about the two 'lights' - the remaining 'planets'* , Sun and Moon? We now face another task: we need to work with a seven sided star to illustrate a further vital link between Stonehenge and ancient cosmology. Placing all seven planets in the order of their relative maximum velocities as observed from the Earth (a geocentric model), we arrive at the following order:-

The Planets placed in order of their Maximum Angular Velocity, as viewed from the Earth	
Moon	Thirteen degrees a day (average)
Mercury	Two degrees a day
Venus	Just over one degree a day
Sun	Just under one degree a day
Mars	Always under one degree a day
Jupiter	About Thirty degrees a year
Saturn	About Thirteen degrees a year

This table is *exactly* the order of the planets which would be produced by an observer of the night sky. The regular changes in the skies catalogued by naked eye observation over many year would produce the planetary order given.

---

* The word *Planet* comes from the Greek word for *wanderer*, something the Sun and Moon both do a lot of when viewed from the Earth - i.e. geocentrically observed.

Placing these in cyclic order around the perimeter of a seven-sided star or *heptagram* we can now discover the inner astronomic meaning behind the Genesis creation story, through the order of the days of the week.

Thus it is that one of the oldest extant Bible texts, taken from a Sumerian creation story which is known to have its roots beyond the advent of writing, contains a geometric function which cannot be accidental and which connects us straight back with the relationship between the Aubrey and Sarsen circles at Stonehenge. The sevenfold motif (7 X 8 = 56) leads to a star whose inner core contains the Sarsen circle. This seven sided star is fundamental to understanding the architecture of the two main phases of Stonehenge - see figure 11 on page 26.

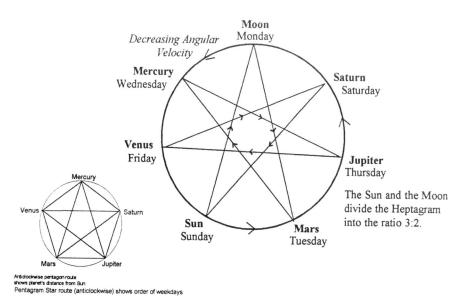

Figure 30. The Pentagram Function and the Five visible Planets; Figure 31. The Days of the Week related to the angular velocities of the Seven Visible Planets - i.e. including the Sun and Moon - via the Heptagram 'Star'.

We must return to our study of the pentagram star. The lunation pentagram provides a direct link between the number 13 (if this is taken as the enclosing circle diameter) and the number of lunations within a solar year. Remembering this shape, plus the order of the days of the week - i.e. the *planets*, would have allowed an apprentice astronomer/priest to memorise quickly the order of the five true planets and to predict lunar phases. Using a pentagram in this way would have meant proportioning down the 12.368 lunations (the 'star arm' length) onto a solar year rope.

Divorced from the lunation triangle, this can be of any unit length one chooses. It is, of course, perfectly possible to proportion the lunation length onto the 13 unit diameter of the enclosing circle, the diameter then representing the solar year. If this is assumed then each 'star arm' of the pentagram has a length which coincides with the number of days in the EclipseYear (accuracy within 0.2%). This is an another remarkable geometric 'coincidence', for we can now state:

> The Pentagram 'star' offers *all* the geometric information to allow accurate prediction of lunar phases and eclipses. If the diameter of the enclosing circle is taken to be 13 units, then the 'star arms' each have a length equal to the annual lunations (12.364). If the diameter is then taken to represent the solar year of 365.242 days, then each 'star arm' has a length corresponding to 346.2 days, which is the Eclipse Year.

We now understand the importance these two key lengths 12 and 13 offer in astronomical prediction as well as in making calendar choices. The ratio 12:13 may be found at Stonehenge to an accuracy of 0.2%. The diameter of the Aubrey circle compared to the distance between the Aubrey centre and the Heel Stone forms the ratio 13:12. The Station Stone rectangle has its longer sides equal to 12 units if, once again, the Aubrey circle is assumed to have a diameter of 13 units.

Does a pentagram star fit into Stonehenge? Not quite, we would need 55 and not 56 Aubrey holes for that, although a passable pentagram may be made using the Aubrey holes; the Sarsen circle holding the inner pentagon. However, the motive to construct a pentagram *star* would have fitted everything else we have been discussing.

Whatever all this may ultimately mean, it is surely very interesting material to ponder. Neolithic man, in Europe, deliberately built megalithic monuments which derive from pentagonal forms. We have already looked at one of these, the compound ring *Moel ty Uchaf*. He also inscribed pentagrams within stone circles, contemporary with the building of Stonehenge I, for the double ring at Clava contains one, as discovered recently by Anne Macauley (figure 34). Again, one must face the fact that ancient Europeans were working out and applying extremely sophisticated geometrical and astronomical ideas at least some 500 years before the architect of the Great Pyramid was born and 2700 years before Greek philosophers reinvented much of it. Again, we must refute the implication that some of them were indeed as barbaric as history tells us they were. We must again and again ask the difficult question: where did the source of this knowledge originate?

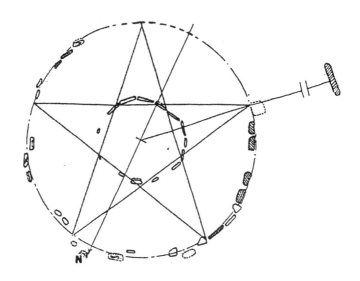

Figure 34. Miltown of Clava (Pentagram) Double Ring
(By kind permission of Anne Macauley and Gordon Strachan)

Thus, the pentagram/pentagon appears to have once assumed a very important role in megalithic thought and, hence, in Earth-based astronomy. The simple functions described here would have enabled a megalith builder to perform all his or her normal duties merely through remembering a beautiful and simple geometric shape. It is totally apposite that this shape embodies the number *phi* throughout its geometry - like lettering through a stick of sea-side rock. The number of evolution and growth permeates out of almost every dimension and proportion of the five sided form.

There are many books written about the geometry and mathematical aspects of this shape, although none of them describe the links with Sun, Moon, Earth astronomy given above. *The Divine Proportion* by H.E.Huntley (Dover) provides a superb account of just how special the pentagram is, showing its apparently infinite links with the so-called *'Golden Section'* number *phi* (the irrational number 1.618033989...) and hence the Fibonacci series. This number and this mathematical series occur throughout nearly every evolutionary process, from the shape of a snail's shell to the way branches and flowers form on a plant. Artists and architects incorporate the ratio phi : 1 within their work in order to achieve harmony and balance. The Greek Parthenon is one example of *phi* applied in human endeavours. This same ratio may be found in the breeding of animals, the generational patterns of bees and, as we shall now discover, the relationship between the orbits of Venus and the Earth.

- *Venus and The Divine Proportion* -

The planet Venus has an orbital period of 224.7 days, whilst that of the Earth is 365.24 days. Punch these numbers into a calculator and divide the larger by the smaller. You will get an answer very close (0.5%) to *phi*. Furthermore, Venus periodically appears to stop in the sky and then *retrograde* or go backwards against the backdrop of the fixed stars. This happens every 584 days (the Mayan number *par excellence*) and 584/365 also yields *phi* to 0.5% accuracy. This phenomenon of the retrograding of Venus, observed over 8 years, makes the planet trace out a pentagram star in the heavens; a most beautiful display by the planet to whom astrologers have always ascribed the qualities of harmony and relationship is shown below (figure 32). Perhaps you have just found out why.

We must look a little more deeply into this relationship between harmony, the number five, the 5:12:13 triangle, the planet Venus and the irrational number *phi*. For those people who are superstitious, there is the ominous recurrence, from time to time, of the 13th day of one of the 12 months falling on a Friday. Friday the 13th is said to be very unlucky. For Friday (Freya, Frigga, Venus) substitute the 5th day of the Week and you have 5, 12 and 13 placed right in front of your eyes **as a warning of something to be avoided**. This superstition runs right through our consciousness even in our modern 'rational' world.

Whether this stems from patriarchal suppression of ancient calendrical practices or from keepers of the sacred knowledge isn't clear, although the hidden message is beautifully clear once we understand the cargo contained within the lunation triangle.

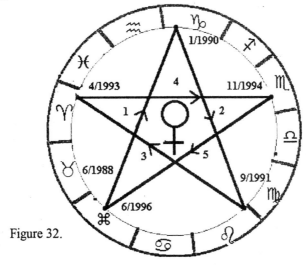

Figure 32.

- *Stonehenge, Lunations and the Musical Scale* -

Another fascinating glimpse of the cosmic principles surrounding the lunation triangle and hence Stonehenge comes from a study of music. The history of harmony and music are anchored very firmly within cosmology. We think, in total error, that modern musical science has replaced the curious ideas of the Hindus, Pythagoreans and all those other quaint folk[13], and we think that we *never* think of music in terms of cosmic principles nor relate the two. But look closely at the modern piano keyboard (figure 33). To complete the octave, there are 13 semitones and 12 intervals. The chromatic scale isn't complete without the octave. The name given to the note which precedes the octave - the leading note - indicates the sense of incompleteness if that completing (*thirteenth*) octave note isn't played.

Figure 33. The Piano Keyboard

This interplay of 12 and 13 in the chromatic scale allows a musician to modulate (change key) into any other key without the howling discords formed from non equal-tempered instruments. The musical scale contains *seven* separate notes yet needs the *eighth* to complete the scale, just as the chromatic scale contains *twelve* separate tones yet needs the *thirteenth*, octave note, to complete the scale. Here we find a direct connection between the sevenfold and eightfold nature of the Aubrey circle and the, by now, familiar connection between 12 and 13. Meanwhile, humankind has determined that the 'black notes' on the keyboard, which must be five in number, are predictably although astonishingly arranged in the ratio 3:2.

---

[13] See *The Myth of Invariance* by Ernest G. McClain (Shambhala, 1978). *The origin of the Gods, Mathematics and Music from the Rig Veda to Plato.* Not an easy read, but a wonderful seminal text on music and cosmology.

> **The modern keyboard which allows (musical) harmony to be found is a derivative of the 5:12:13 lunation triangle .**

Was the design of the keyboard conceived of consciously or was it the inevitable form by which musical harmony can be best expressed? Did man unconsciously respond to the rhythms of the Sun and Moon? It is only recently that the equal tempered scale has emerged as a moderately tolerable solution to the age old problem of key modulation in music. Was the design always waiting for conscious expression, with man eventually aligning himself to the inevitable form it must take? Profound questions indeed!

Chapter Five

- *Stonehenge - A New Phase* -

However strange all these connections and 'coincidences' may appear, taken together they allow one to glimpse something about ancient thought which, in our modern scientific age, we appear to have lost. That something is *holism*, for, in all of the material we have studied, we find no separation between science and religion, between architecture and astronomy nor between Man and the Cosmos. Throughout my work to date, I am continually drawn to the sublime attractiveness of this 'seamless garment' of evolution. Instead of all the '-ologies' and '-isms' of our fragmented arts and sciences, I would like to see their little compartments dissolved, being replaced by a single theme - *integration*. If the emerging science and art which comes out of these pages has to be given a name, then I would call it *Geocosmology*. Rudolph Steiner, over a century ago, termed it *anthroposophy*.

The previous section illustrated some of the stranger aspects of Stonehenge and its siting which face any researcher looking for a better model of ancient history than that to be currently found in the history books. My own work consists of rediscoveries of a corpus of information which appears to form a remarkably consistent cosmology. Almost nothing is known concerning its cultural origins, spread of use nor why it petered out. The discoveries here form a key which begins to unlock a different history, a more convincing one than the prevalent 'woad-covered savages attempting to make better pots' approach. I hope that I have shaken this popularly held view of the primitive status of human life in neolithic Britain, for at least a proportion of the population clearly had their minds set on more profound things. Stonehenge did not build itself.

The contents of this book, taken together, tell a fascinating tale which has waited far too long to be told. Ever since Alex Thom and Gerald Hawkins rocked the archaeological world in the '50's' and '60's' there has been a very uneasy peace, an expectation of change concerning our knowledge of the origins and purposes of Stonehenge.

There have been two main categories for books about Stonehenge. There have been the scientific books, which usually and increasingly take the format, '*1001 Things Stonehenge isn't*' without exploring what it might be, and there have been the '*New Age*' books, where reason usually yields to wild speculation. These two categories are poles apart and can never meet, like the two cultures which spawn them. In fact, where these cultures do attempt to meet we observe some of the most difficult social discord seen in Britain during modern times. Perfectly appropriately **and** with perfect timing **and** at exactly the right location, this discord occurs every year at the summer solstice at Stonehenge. Each side of the polarity - scientific materialism against 'New Age' alternative culture - battles with the other in the immediate vicinity of the monument. And, like all polarities, each pole needs something of what the other has in order to neutralise the destructive emotional reactions which well up. The establishment needs to embrace aspects of the new culture and permit other lifestyles and values to co-exist within the country whilst the 'travellers' need to organise themselves better in order that they may put their case for a permanent festival site more convincingly. If one was to read that, in some far off land, armed police were preventing ordinary folk from entering their national temple and arresting them violently if they even approached it, what would you think? Yet this situation occurs with nauseating regularity every year in England and needs to be understood for what it actually represents. Any book on Stonehenge which fails to note this annual event, related, as are *all* the various phases of Stonehenge, to the solstitial sunrise, is incomplete without this contemporary human phase - *Stonehenge V.*

The so-called scientific books tend to be largely unreadable by ordinary folk, due, in the main, to the quite dreadful presentational styles adopted by many academics. There are sins of omission and avoidance of the really sticky questions the monument throws up. Meanwhile, the alternative category of book varies from the downright silly, where great hypotheses are put forward although none are proved or proveable ('*Stonehenge is a UFO*' was one example of the *genre*), to the inspirational and emotive - which can be spiritually uplifting but may never help humankind to discover their practical legacy from Stonehenge. I hope that this book begins a process of bringing the two ends of this polarity together and healing this schism.

Dr Gerald Hawkins found only too well the inflexible attitude adopted by the British establishment towards the acceptance of his new ideas. In modern parlance, he was 'rubbished'. However, he adopted some of the same intolerance when, shortly after the publication of his epic *Stonehenge Decoded* in 1965 (Doubleday), he received a letter from an Englishman or woman in which was stated, "*The numerical structure and geometry of Stonehenge gave a preview of Christianity*". Hawkins found such a comment "odd" and ignored it, but who was the writer? Perhaps we could be 30 years further along the road that leads to the explanation of Stonehenge if Hawkins had pursued this single letter? The moral is surely to embrace all sources of information, however unscientific they may appear, in order to discover the real meaning of Stonehenge.

This book attempts to bring elements of both conventional science and 'New Age' thought together. For every topic and theme, I have attempted to provide a readable text and a set of reasons, mathematical where possible, for any conclusions I have reached. However, I believe that people should prove for themselves any new theory or hypothesis and for this reason, I have included, in addition to the practical applications given earlier, a number of appendices which will assist an interested reader in checking my maths and observations. I only hope you enjoy the same sense of fulfilment that accompanied me throughout my exploration of this material.

Whatever else this text achieves, it surely opens up connecting links between Stonehenge and other sites. It links the monument with other aspects of ancient scientific endeavour and shows a common theme which reached full fruition before and through the original Christian message. The reader now has a much better grasp of why the pentagram (and the number 13) held such a strong influence within the ancient traditions, and why it was made the subject of derision, superstition, fear and persecution, for it is this shape alone which connects the astronomical realities of life on Earth with the number of evolution and growth - *phi*. The establishment, then as now, inherrently avoids looking at the simple truths such things suggest. It has cut itself off from the cosmos.

The Genesis creation story provides clear evidence that its writers understood perfectly well the geometric and astronomical relationships described here. The Babylonian *Enuma Elish* formed part of a cosmology which our modern Bible does not explain. There could only be two reasons for this; the later scribes did not want their readers to understand such matters and/or they were insufficiently cultured to understand just what was thinly hidden just below the surface of this ancient story they were poaching. Either way, it is clear that the translators *were less civilised than the original authors* and this should be taken very seriously for our western culture stems from this very story...*In the beginning..* implies *at the beginning of our current era*. That era began many hundreds of years *after* the ditch and bank were constructed at Stonehenge.

At the very roots of our western culture lies an ignorance and denial of this ancient wisdom, through the evident censorship, persecution and annihilation of all matters appertaining to the Moon (and hence women's importance within society) and the holistic connections which exist between Mankind and the Cosmos. As such, our culture is anti-life and is infected with a *virus* which prevents us from reconnecting to the simple truths, astronomical, numerical and geometrical, which surround us. Like a computer virus, we are prevented from operating the entire program, seeing the bigger vision of life and hence we cannot function properly. *A Key to Stonehenge* suggests that we can eradicate this original error implanted within our thinking, an error placed there some four thousand years ago by person or persons unknown to us and for reasons which are only vaguely understood.

Stonehenge has become **the** symbol of the discord between patriarchal and matriarchal values. Ironically, I believe that it was conceived and built in order to demonstrate quite the reverse; how humankind could bring together the two sides of this duality within a harmonious 'sacred marriage'. It is probably the most sacred monument we have, a fact which English Heritage might do well to consider before turning the temple even more completely into the hands of the moneychangers. I have shown here that it is not a Pagan monument, in the sense that its message is in any way divorced from original Christian sentiments. When 'Stone-killer' Robinson and his anti-pagan crew mounted regular expeditions to topple pagan stones, it was their own lack of balance which was exposed. There is nothing 'evil' or 'devilish' about Stonehenge, although it exposes these sides of our present culture. Nothing horrible is going to happen to anyone if they attempt to become more conscious of what the megalithic builders were trying to understand. Stonehenge represents the commencement of Man's attempts to unite, some would say re-unite, with the Cosmos, to find harmony and meaning, and this process led naturally to the message of Christianity as well as to some other religions.

The pentagram 'star', the heptagram 'star', the 'lunar triangles', the Aubrey holes, and the number 'families' we have seen emerging through the adoption of a 364 day calendar device, all connect the Sun, Moon and planets with life processes on the Earth. These shapes, these celestial bodies, these numbers, and the ratios between them, have all been seen to consistently relate to *phi*, the Fibonacci series, the Earth's axial tilt and to ancient monuments.*

Stonehenge reflects and incorporates these immutable numbers, shapes, and ratios - these were then and are now the design codes for the evolution of life on Earth. This monument, along with certain others which survive in Egypt, Central America and elsewhere tell us something about a cultural aspiration or a striving which modern man has either chosen to forget or is totally unaware of. That *something* connects humankind to the skies and thus to the realities of the cosmos. *As Above, So Below* ran the oracle - and there is a great wisdom to be found in Stonehenge, for it is, at root, a temple dedicated to the creative force within the cosmos, which in our era some still call God.

---

* The Earth's axial tilt and its relationship to human history may be explored in *Hamlet's Mill*, by Giorgio de Santillana and Hertha von Dechend. Published by Gambit (1969).

Additional Reading

In addition to those texts indicated by footnotes, the following books provide valuable additional material relating to *A Key to Stonehenge* :

1. *Stonehenge Complete* by Christopher Chippindale. (Thames and Hudson)

2. *Pi in the Sky* (Counting, Thinking and Being) by Professor John D Barrow.
(Oxford University Press)

3. *The Book of Enoch* translated by R H Charles. (SPCK)

4. *The Gospel of John* by G H C Macgregor. (Hodder and Stoughton)

5. *Christ and the Cosmos* by Gordon Strachan (Labarum Publications, Edinburgh)

6. *Circles and Standing Stones* by Evan Hadingham (Book Club Associates)

7. *The Lost Books of the Bible* (2 Enoch). New American Library (Meridian)

8. *Return of the Goddess* by Edward C Whitmont MD (Arkana)

9. *Serpent in the Sky* by John Antony West. (Julian Press)

10. *Pi in the Sky* by Michael Poynder (Rider). Same title as 2. Very different!

11. *Sun-Moon Integration* by Robin Heath. *Kindred Spirit* magazine.(Vol 2 No 12
and part two in Vol 3 No 1)

12. *The Greek Myths* Vol I and II. by Robert Graves (Penguin)

13. *The Old Straight Track* by Alfred Watkins. (Garnstone Press reprint)

14. *Stonehenge* by R J C Atkinson (Pelican) Highly recommended but very litle
astronomic content.

15. *The Stonehenge People* by Aubrey Burl. (J Dent) See text for details

16. *The Stone Circles of the British Isles* by Aubrey Burl (Yale UP)

17. *Megalithic Remains in Britain and Brittany* by A Thom and A S Thom
(Clarendon)
Works by Fred Hoyle, C A Newham and R S Newall provide good material on the astronomy and placing of Stonehenge. This list is far from exclusive!

- APPENDICES -

Appendix 1 :- Geodetic information.

The form of the Earth cannot be precisely defined mathematically. The Earth's shape is a flattened spheroid (oblate sphere), and the best representation of its shape is taken to be an ellipsoid of rotation. There are a number of these, which makes precise results with the material in this book impossible. The so-called Airy spheroid gives the best 'fit' for the area around the British Isles and is the one used for calculations here. Here are the figures for the Earth, with the dimensions in miles shown in brackets:-

	Airy Spheroid (UK)	**International (1924)**
Major Semi-axis (a)	6377.563396Km (3962.94252)	6378.388000Km (3963.45492)
Minor Semi-axis (b)	6356.256910Km (3949.70292)	6356.911946Km (3950.10995)

These yield the following data about the Earth :-

Circumference (a)	40071.41263Km (24899.9022)	40076.59377Km (24903.1217)
(b)	39937.54003Km (24816.7154)	39941.65574Km (24819.2728)

Appendix 2 :- Units of Measurement

The metric system defines the metre as being one ten-millionth part of the distance from either pole to the equator, *around the circumference* (i.e. one quadrant). This distance is almost impossible to accurately evaluate because the Earth is not a true sphere. In 1795, the mathematician Collet outlined a more scientifically valid unit, that based on one ten-millionth of the distance *from the centre of the Earth to one of the two poles*. This "Collet" unit has a dimension of 25.0265 British inches (0.6357m). But this same dimension occurs five times - to four decimal places of accuracy - within the Great Pyramid at important constructional interfaces. It is called the *Sacred Cubit*. Furthermore, there are at least four places within the Pyramid where an exact one-twenty-fifth subdivision may be found, this offering the derivation of the so-called *Primitive Inch*. This is equal to *just* over the current British inch - 1.00106 British inches. The relationship between the *Primitive Inch* and the Solar year may be found several times within the Pyramid (eg the King's Chamber contains two examples - 365.242P" and 116.26P" - this last number being the exact diameter of a 'year circle' having a perimeter of 365.242P"). All of these examples suggest that a researcher might benefit from translating the metric dimensions of surveyed megalithic monuments into inches in order to facilitate the understanding of their astronomic meanings.

The other major unit used by the Egyptians was the Royal Cubit of 20.6284..+ British inches. Measuring sticks of this unit still survive - there are two in the Louvre - and this length defined the Egyptian unit of area, the *Aroura*, which is the area of a square whose sides are 100 Royal Cubits in length. Now, one quarter of the *Aroura* is also the area of a circle having as its circumference the number of Primitive Inches equal to ten times the number of days in the solar (tropical) year. Horapollon writes that: *'To represent the current year they (the Egyptians) depict the fourth part of an Aroura.'*

There are some quite tantalising connections between these units. For example, I have noticed that the Royal Cubit forms a ratio to Alex Thom's Megalithic Yard which is almost 1:*phi*. The Megalithic Yard is 2.72 feet, curiously near the value of the physical constant e. Much more research needs to be done in order to understand better any apparently unified unit system held by the ancient world.

Appendix 3 : Time Measurements

It is interesting that, expressed in miles, the circumference of the Earth is just under 25,000 miles. Because there are 24 hours within the day, we could speculate that the mile may originally have been defined such that 24,000 of them made up the circumference. This represents a solar 'day' unit - 24 divides by 12. Taking the conversion ratio from the figures quoted in appendix 4 we get 0.965 (mean). Applying this to the 5:12:13 Preseli-Stonehenge triangle we then get distances in 'Circumference Miles' between each point which correspond to exactly ten times the triangle's ratios. The lunation triangle is thus confirmed by the distances, and the suggested unit comes from the triangle.

However, the precessional year, caused by the interaction of the Moon and the Earth, is almost 26,000 years long. This number, as a multiple of 13, is decidedly lunar and offers another unit for the mile - the 'Precessional Mile'. Here the ratio becomes 1.046, making the Preseli-Stonehenge triangle return distances which very closely represent the lunar orbit triangle.

It is very interesting that the current British Mile sits halfway between these two rather obvious ways of relating cosmic cycles to the rotating Earth. The fact that the Preseli-Stonehenge triangle produces either the lunation or the lunar orbit triangle, in terms of these two modified mile units, when one takes either the solar (12) day or the lunar-caused precessional year (13), should align us to possible intended standards of length in use. The reader should note that all of this suggests that some people knew that the Earth was round way before 2000 bc.

Appendix 4 : Earth Polygons

Every simple regular polygon may be formed using the poles and the equator, plus the addition of the Pyramid site and Stonehenge-Preseli. This may readily be shown to be true if one considers the semicircle defined by the two poles; the triangle by the south pole with the Pyramid at 30 degrees north; the square by the poles and the equator; the pentagon by taking the Preseli-Stonehenge-Giza Great Circle, whence the Preseli site lies 72 degrees from the equatorial 'cut' of the circle; the hexagon may be formed by making the double triangle. The septagon is suggested by the latitude of the Preseli site from the equator (52 degrees). The Arctic circles and Tropics form an octagon (within a degree); the nonagon can be formed by taking the limits of sunrise and sunset azimuths from their equinoctial positions) only at the latitude of Stonehenge (40 degrees). A decagon may be formed from the longitude difference between Preseli and the Pyramid site, which is less than one quarter of a degree short of 36 degrees. This same shape is suggested from the Preseli - Giza Great Circle. From the equator, Giza lies about 36 degrees along the circle; Preseli at 72 degrees. Try locating all of these with a globe! The Great Circle distance between Giza and Stonehenge is 2238 miles; Stonehenge to the Preseli Bluestone site 135 miles.

Appendix Five :- ASTRONOMIC CONSTANTS

Solar Year - Tropical (SY) $= 365.2422$ days $(0.985807^0$ per day)

Lunar Month (lunation period LM) $= 29.53059$ days (average figure)
(The Moon moves an average 13.15347^0 per day)

Lunar Synodic Orbital Period (LOP) $= 27.322$ days (average figure)

Lunations in one Solar Tropical Year (L) $= 12.368$ (S/LM)

Lunar Orbits in one Solar Tropical Year (Geocentric) $= 13.379$ (S/LOP)

Earth's axial tilt angle (e) in degrees (1990) $= 23.45$ (3000 bc $= 24.03$)

Precessional Year (approximate, it varies from century to century and from book to book) $= 25,920$ years

Angular tilt of Moon's orbital plane (i), in degrees $= 5.14$

12 lunations (**Lunar Year**) period $= 12$ x LM $= 354.36708$ days (**LY**)

13 lunar orbits (**Lunar Orbital Year**) period $= 13$ x LOP $= 355.186$ days

Eclipse Year (Elapsed time between Sun's path intersecting the Lunar north node)
$= 346.62$ days (**EY**)
Eclipse 'Season' $=$ Eclipse Year/2 $= 173.3$ days ± 17 days

Moon's nodes rotational period around zodiac (clockwise) $= 18.61$ years
- (18.61 x $18.61 = 346.33 =$ Eclipse Year to 0.084%)

Annual angular movement of Moon's nodes in degrees $= 19.34$

DERIVED CONSTANTS REFERRED TO IN THE TEXT

Lunar Year / Solar Year $= 0.97023$ (LY/SY)

Eclipse Year / Solar Year $= 0.94902$ (EY/SY)

$\dfrac{\text{Lunar Orbital Month}}{\text{Lunar Month}} = 0.92521$ (LOP/LM)

Precessional Year /12 (*An 'Age'*) $= 2160$ years

ASTRONOMIC CONSTANTS TO BE FOUND WITHIN THE 'LUNAR TRIANGLES'

(a) The 'Lunation' Triangle

Lunation Hypotenuse = 12.369 units (cf. 12.368 lunations[L])
[Accuracy to 0.01%]

'12' side/12.369 lunation hypotenuse = 0.97017

(cf. Lunar Year/Solar year LY/SY = 0.97023 [0.006%])

Lunation hypotenuse/'13' hypotenuse = 0.95146

(cf. Eclipse Year/Solar Year EY/SY = 0.949015 [to 0.26%])

(b) The Lunar Orbit Triangle

Lunar Orbit Hypotenuse = 13.3686 (cf. 13.379 LOPs)
[accuracy to 0.07%]

(c) The Eclipse Year Triangle

$$\frac{\text{Hypotenuse length}}{\text{'12' length}} = \frac{11.3701}{12.0000} = \frac{EY}{SY} \quad [\text{ to } 0.15\%]$$

ASTRONOMIC CONSTANTS TO BE FOUND WITHIN THE PENTAGRAM 'STAR'

'Star' Arm length / Diameter of enclosing circle = 0.95108

(cf. Eclipse Year / Solar Year EY/SY = 0.949015 [0.22% accurate]

If enclosing circle is 13 units in diameter, then the 'star' arm length is 12.364.
This, compared to a 12 unit length offers the Lunar Year / Solar Year
(0.97023) directly. [accuracy 0.025%]

OTHER ASTRONOMIC CONSTANTS OF INTEREST

$$\frac{\text{Lunar Month Period}}{\text{Lunar Orbital Period}} = \frac{1.080836}{} \quad : \quad \frac{13}{12} = 1.08333+$$

IMPORTANT CONSTANTS FOUND AT MEGALITHIC SITES REFERRED TO IN THE TEXT

(figures in brackets multiply the figures by '*pi*'- see page 54 ⌐)
[figures in square brackets indicate error from correspondence]

STONEHENGE

Aubrey hole diameter (87.8 m) compared to perimeter of Sarsen
circle (inner face 93.3 m)   = 0.9389 = EY/SY [to 1.06%].

MOEL TY UCHAF
(after Thom)

$$\frac{\text{Perimeter of Moel ty Uchaf}}{\text{Defining Circle perimeter}} = \frac{43.98MY}{42.85MY} = 0.97431 \ [+0.41\%]$$

FLATTENED CIRCLES
(after Thom)

$$\frac{\text{Perimeter of 'Type A' flattened circle}}{\text{Defining circle perimeter}} = 0.9737 \ (3.0591) \ [+0.4\%]$$

$$\frac{\text{Perimeter of 'Type B' flattened circle}}{\text{Defining circle perimeter}} = 0.9568 \ (2.9572) \ [+0.78\%]$$

COMPUTER PROGRAMS AVAILABLE FROM BLUESTONE PRESS

1. SOLAR RISE AND SET AZIMUTHS. Lists for each day or each
month.   Does not account for parallax or refraction effects and
assumes a level horizon. Allows the Earth's axial tilt (e) to be altered,
allowing simulation of ancient conditions. Supplied with graph of
variation of e with time.

2. SPHERICAL GEOMETRY PROGRAM. Enter latitude and
longitude for two locations and the program gives the Great Circle
distance between them, along with other information.

Both programs written in BASIC.
Listings £2.00 each (include SAE)